HIROSHIGE

HIROSHIGE

A Hundred Views of Edo

Mikhail Uspensky

BARNES & NOBLE BOOKS

NEW YORK

Text: Mikhail Uspensky
Layout: Baseline Co Ltd

© 2005 Confidential Concepts, Worldwide, USA

This edition published by Barnes & Noble, Inc.
by arrangement Sirrocco-Parkstone International

2005 Barnes & Noble Books

M 10 9 8 7 6 5 4 3 2 1

ISBN 0-7607-7291-6

Printed in China

Contents

1. Kitagawa Utamaro. 1754-1806
Carving the Woodblocks
From a composition of six prints
*Making Edo's Famous Souvenir the
Full-Colour Print. Ca.* 1800

2. Detail of a key-block

The series *Mcisho Edo Hyakkci* - usually translated as *A Hundred Famous Views of Edo* - occupies a special place both in the artistic biography of Ando Hiroshige (1797-1858) and in the history of Japanese xylography as a whole. Printing as a means of reproducing an image was known in Japan as early as the eighth century, but it emerged as an art form in its own right considerably later - in the second half of the seventeenth century. That period was marked by the formation of a new urban culture reflecting the tastes of the third and fourth estates, merchants and craftsmen who were playing an even greater role in the economic and, as time went on, cultural life of the country. Between the seventeenth and nineteenth centuries, the Edo period (1603-1868), a new tendency in urban art developed and it is to this style, known as *ukiyo-e*, literally "pictures of the floating world", that the woodblock print belongs. The primary subject matter was the lives of the city dwellers themselves, the daily round and festivals.

The founder of the *ukiyo-e* woodblock print is considered to have been Hishikawa Moronobu (*ca.* 1618-1694), who was the first to produce not only book illustrations but also works intended to stand

on their own. In the seventeenth century and on into the first half of the eighteenth, prints were mainly black and white. They were produced from a single block of wood known as the "keyblock". As early as the beginning of the eighteenth century, though, a desire to increase the chromatic scope of the prints led them to be hand-tinted first with one colour, then with two and three. At that time (customarily known as the early or primitive period) the range of subjects was established and genres came into being. The most popular genres throughout the history of the woodblock print were *bijin-ga* and *yakusha-e*.

Bijin-ga translates as "depictions of beauties" and such works did indeed depict the attractive *denizens* of the "green quarters" as the Japanese, in imitation of their Chinese neighbours, called those parts of the city, which in Europe became known as the "red-light district". In the period in question, the "green quarters" played a significant role in the lives of the Japanese as a consequence of the peculiar political situation in the country. Japan in the seventeenth to nineteenth centuries was a police state in the full sense of the expression. All aspects of social and personal life were strictly regimented.

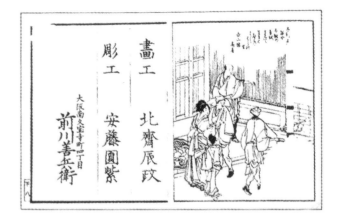

3. Hosoki Toshiichi
Producing Full-Colour Woodblock Prints
From the series *Mirror of Various Artisan
Trades*. 1890

4. Katsushika Hokusai. 1760–1849
Yoshiwara
Keyblock print and extant woodblock for
the end-page of the book *A Look Along
Both Banks of the River Sumida* (re-carving
for the 19th-century edition)

In that atmosphere of constant control, the "green quarters" became a kind of no-man's land, a place where modes of behaviour and interaction between people were not dictated from above, where a city dweller might, if only for a time, feel himself unconstrained and independent. People came here to attend *Kabuki* theatre performances, to make business deals and, of course, to visit the teahouses whose geisha hostesses were famous not only for their beauty, but also for their education, their refined taste and exquisite manners. That is why the *bijin-ga* genre became one of the main elements of *ukiyo-e*.

At a time when there were no mass media, woodblock prints, including *bijin-ga*, assumed something of their function, in an imperfect and, more often than not, indirect form. They informed people about certain aspects of life in the capital, about fashions, more precisely about the fabrics fashionable for female attire in the current season, about the leading figures of the "green quarters", sometimes about the daughters of merchants or craftsmen whose beauty had become the talk of the city, and so on. In the overwhelming majority of cases, *bijin-ga* served as an advertisement, not so much for a specific woman as for the establishment in which she served. Although the name of the person depicted would be

included in the print, it was not her real one: the name of the "leading lady" of a teahouse was passed down from one individual to another. The most prominent beauties in the large establishments were very likely to share the same *nom de guerre*.

The aspect of individual advertising was stronger in another genre of the woodblock print - *yakusha-e* (depictions of actors). Such works are primarily portraits of performers from the capital's theatres who enjoyed incomparable popularity with their audiences.

These two genres, as has been said, remained dominant throughout the age of the woodblock print. The stylistic approach did change, influenced by a number of factors, most often connected with the cultural life of the city and the activities of the *ren* - literary or poetic societies of city dwellers. One of these *ren* is associated with an event of exceptional importance in the history of the woodblock print - the appearance of the colour print around the beginning of 1766, an "invention" traditionally attributed to Suzuki Harunobu (1724-1770). In point of fact, the colour print had been known considerably earlier, at least since the early seventeenth century. It was, however, Harunobu who first used the technique in *ukiyo-e* and who used it for a large print-run.

5. Utagawa Toyohiro. 1773-1828
The Third Month
Triptych from the series *The Twelve Months Jointly Pictured by Toyokuni and Toyohiro. Ca.* 1801

Printing in colour from woodblocks is a laborious business and requires the collaboration of several specialists: the artist who produces a sketch of the future print; a craftsman who "developed" the sketch to such a degree of detail that a block could be cut from it; another who transferred the image onto blocks of wood cut along the grain, a separate block being required for each colour; and a printer who worked by hand, without using a printing-press. The publisher usually had a very important role to play; he not only exercised overall control and dealt with the sale of the prints, but quite often came up with the idea for a work. There may have been another contributor – a poet who composed a verse to accompany the print and, in some cases, acted as a calligrapher writing his piece on the sketch himself.

Late in 1764, Harunobu produced *egoyomi*, or illustrated calendars, printed in several colours. They were intended for members of the Kikurensha society, which was led by Okubo Jinshiro, Harunobu's friend and educator. The difference between these works and everything that the artist had created before lay not so much in the printing technique as in the interpretation of the subjects. The stylistic approach and the choice of accompanying verse clearly betray an attempt to turn the "low-born" art of *ukiyo-e* into something comparable with the classical art of the Heian period (794-1185). The attempt failed, but the refinement of Harunobu's style set the tone for the development of the woodblock print over the rest of the century and into the next. The second half of the eighteenth century saw the emergence, in the work of such artists as Kitagawa Utamaro (1754-1806), Torii Kiyonaga (1752-1815) and

Toshusai Sharaku (active 1794-95), of new variants of the *bijin-ga* and *yakusha-e* which represented a consistent development of the ideas generated by Harunobu and his circle, that included Katsukawa Shunsho (1726-1792), Ippitsusai Buncho (active 1765–92) and Isoda Koryushai (active 1764-1788). This period is reckoned to be the heyday of *ukiyo-e* art. The first half and middle of the nineteenth century was its final period, a time when a new generation of artists appeared on the scene.

Bijin-ga and *yakusha-e* remained the leading genres, but they developed along different lines from those seen in the eighteenth century. The greatest artists, Utagawa Toyokuni (1769-1825), Hosoda Eishi (1756-1829), Rekisentei Eiri (active 1790-1800) and Keisai Eisen (1790-1848), created works as good as those of the 1780s and 1790s, but aimed at the viewer of the new era. These works possess their own distinctive brand of expressiveness, which enables them to compete with earlier works. In late *bijin-ga* the same subjects are presented in a different idiom – realistic, one might say "earthier" than before.

In the 1830s and 1840s lifeless, eclectic prints appeared with even greater frequency. In these works purely formal concerns and a penchant for superficial effects supplanted the subtle conveying of the model's mood, which had been arguably the most salient quality of prints in the second half of the eighteenth century.

Symptoms of decline became fully obvious later, in the period known as Bakumatsu (1853-1867), which preceded the Meiji revolution of 1868. Thus the use of the term "decline" with reference to all the first half and middle of the century is hardly justified. And not only because in the work of Utagawa Kunisada (1786–1864),

Utagawa Kuniyoshi (1797-1861) and others the traditional genres went through their last flowering, but primarily because in this period a genre new for *ukiyo-e* sprang to the fore - *fukei-ga* (landscape).

The acknowledged founder of the *ukiyo-e* landscape print was Katsushika Hokusai (1760-1849), one of the best-known Japanese artists. In terms of type, Hokusai's *ukiyo-e* landscape is unusual for Japanese art. It differs first and foremost from the traditional Far Eastern landscape, which was customarily understood as a reflection of a philosophical view of the world, through far greater attention paid to the real-life appearance of the locality depicted. It is not possible to say, though, that Hokusai himself developed this new concept for Japan from start to finish. The emergence of a new type of landscape in the woodblock print had its pre-history and it is worthwhile examining it briefly, since it helps us to evaluate Hiroshige's contribution to the development of this *ukiyo-e* genre, his innovation and achievements.

Landscape appeared in woodblock prints at almost the same time as the leading *ukiyo-e* genres - the theatrical portrait and depictions of beauties. We first come across landscape prints in the works of one of the greatest artists of the "monochrome" period, Okumura Masanobu (1686-1764). Two tendencies can be distinguished in this sphere of Masanobu's output. One was the product of the artist's attempt to use unchanged the scheme and visual structure of the landscapes of the traditional Kano and Tosa schools in the woodcut print (black and white or hand-tinted). This attempt ended in failure: the landscape prints to a "classical" formula are no more than crude replicas of the painted models.

The second type was "perspective pictures" - *uki-e*, that is, compositions using linear perspective and chiaroscuro (light and shade to model volumes). As a rule, scholars link the penetration of these kinds of devices into Japanese art, and hence the genesis of *uki-e*, with the influence of the European artistic tradition. It cannot be ruled out, however, that the first impulse for the creation of *uki-e* came not straight from Western works, but indirectly from Chinese landscape prints created under the influence of European prototypes. In particular there was a strong influence from the *megane-e* (literally "spectacles pictures"), which were produced in large numbers in the southern Chinese city of Suzhou. Such works were enormously popular in Japan and often shown in a *nozoki-karakuri*, a type of peep show in which the picture was first reflected in a mirror and then viewed through a magnifying glass to intensify the perspective effects and the chiaroscuro, giving the illusion of three-dimensionality. Many noted Japanese painters and graphic artists created *megane-e* in the process of mastering the laws of linear perspective and light-and-shade modelling. Among them were Maruyama Okyo (1733-1795), Shiba Kokan (1747-1818) and Okumura Masanobu himself.

Soon the "perspectivists" gave up imitating Chinese *megane-e* and took as their models the primary source - Dutch copper engravings. The direct turning to the artistic traditions of the West was an important moment in the history of Japanese art, following which, despite all the difficulties, European influence grew steadily stronger. Many phenomena of the Edo period, especially in the realm of the arts, arose through the obvious and significant involvement of the European artistic tradition. This applies to the woodblock print too. The new conception of the landscape as a depiction of a specific locality formed in *ukiyo-e* under the direct

6. Suzuki Harunobu. 1724-1770
Tamagawa River in Takano
From the series *Six Rivers in Tamagawa*

7. Furuyama Moromasa. Ca. 1712-1772
Snowfall by the "Great Gates" of Shin-Yoshiwara

8. Torii Kiyonaga. 1752-1815
Sumidagawa River Ferry
Triptych

influence of European works, first and foremost Dutch etchings, which entered the country, albeit in limited numbers, through Deshima, the Dutch trading post in Nagasaki, which was the sole source for the dissemination of European learning in the Edo period.

A special role in this process was played by *rangaku*, "Dutch studies". After 1720 when the bans on all things European that had been imposed in the early seventeenth century were eased and it became possible to study European learning and art, *rangaku* emerged as a special field of scholarship. It aimed at mastery of all available Western knowledge, including *rangaku-e,* the European manner of painting.

Shiba Kokan, the leading figure of *rangaku-e*, and his followers practised both painting in oils and copper plate engraving. One of the chief themes of the latter was landscape in which the artists employed, with greater or lesser success, methods of constructing an image which were new to them: perspective and the chiaroscuro modelling of shapes. The Western brand of painting held no small attraction: many *ukiyo-e* artists paid tribute to this fascination with European art, including the young Katsushika Hokusai, who studied in Shiba Kokan's studio, Utagawa Toyoharu (1735-1814), the founder of the Utagawa School and the teacher of Utagawa Toyohiro (1773-1828), who was in turn the teacher of Ando Hiroshige.

In the perspective prints produced by Masanobu and his contemporaries – Nishimura Shigenaga (1697[?]-1756), Furuyama Moromasa (*ca.* 1712-1772), Torii Kiyomasu II (1706-1763) and others – depictions of nature as such are not to be found. Most often we see there the interiors of theatres or teahouses, less frequently street scenes, but those too are treated in such a way as to make them more like interiors.

All *uki-e* is marked by exaggerated perspective, with the distant plane being worked as carefully and in as much detail as the foreground. Such prints could be contemplated for a long time. Their entertainment and information value was exceptionally high and that determined the immense popularity of *uki-e* in the first half and middle of the eighteenth century.

Despite the fact that early *uki-e* works cannot be regarded as landscapes in the full sense of the word, the activities of Masanobu, Kokan and their followers represented a first, but highly important step in the formation of the landscape as an independent genre within *ukiyo-e.*

The following stage in the process is associated with Utagawa Toyoharu. His perspective prints differ appreciably from the *uki-e* of the preceding period. While studying the laws of perspective and chiaroscuro, he became the first artist to copy Dutch engravings and also used them in independent compositions with far more assurance than his predecessors. Moreover, Toyoharu was the first to produce polychrome *uki-e*, which considerably enriched the aesthetic power of his work. Finally, in some of them, he succeeded not only in conveying more or less exactly the appearance of the locality depicted, but also to some extent the state of the elements. Such prints of his are typologically close to the *ukiyo-e* landscape proper, which reached its final form only later.

Uki-e, which, were exceptionally popular between 1770 and 1800, had a substantial influence on the traditional *ukiyo-e* woodcut print. Many artists who worked chiefly in the *bijin-ga* and *yakusha-e* genres occasionally tried their hand at "perspective pictures". They included Torii Kiyonaga, Kitagawa Utamaro, Katsukawa Shunsho and Kitao Shigemasa (1739-1820). In the works of these artists we find the first attempt to combine devices characteristic of "perspective pictures" with the decorative qualities of colour woodblock prints.

Even more significant for the development of *ukiyo-e*, however, was the fact that under the influence of *uki-e* artists began to use landscape backgrounds. And although, as a rule, the genre scene and the landscape are disconnected, in the finest works of this type (notably those produced by Kiyonaga) the techniques borrowed from Western art do not seem alien or emphatically exotic (as in early *uki-e*), but rather fit into the structure traditional for the *ukiyo-e* print.

So, the "perspective print" of the second half of the eighteenth century and those elements in *ukiyo-e* which appeared under its influence can be considered the immediate precursors of the *ukiyo-e* landscape as such, which acquired its final form in the work of Hokusai.

In the course of a long life, Hokusai worked in various print genres as well as other forms of art. More specifically, he did not merely pay tribute to the fascination with "perspective pictures" as other print artists did, but, under the guidance of Shiba Kokan, made a study of the Western style of art. In the 1790s Hokusai produced a series of prints, which, despite their creator's obvious indebtedness to Dutch etchings, represent something qualitatively new compared to the *uki-e* of Toyoharu and his followers.

Above all, nature in all its variety had become the main theme of the works. Hokusai's depiction of a locality could be just as topographically accurate as those of his perspectivist predecessors, yet he did not restrict himself to the mere setting-down of a motif from nature, but rather strove to convey his own view of the world, his understanding of the relationship between man and his environment. And finally, Hokusai was the first to be able to combine harmoniously the laws for the perspective construction of space and the linear rhythm that is an inherent feature of the Japanese print. It was with these early works by Hokusai that the history of the landscape genre in *ukiyo-e* began.

In the 1820s, Hokusai produced his most famous landscape series, most notably Thirty-Six Views of Mount Fuji (mid-1820s-early 1830s). His works have something in common with both classical Japanese painting and the eighteenth-century *uki-e*, but at the same time they differ fundamentally from them. The classical Far Eastern landscape in essence ignored the actual appearance of what was being depicted and sought through natural forms to express philosophical ideas about the universe, while in Hokusai's art it is always bound up with a specific locality, the topographical features of which are quite often defined by inscriptions. The specific quality of Hokusai's landscapes differs from that of the eighteenth-century *uki-e* in which the depiction of the natural world did not go beyond the bounds of conscientious, and somewhat lumbering, topographical studies. Hokusai constantly made sketches from life, but in the course of creating a print he processed them, creating a generalized image of nature, that was, however, not speculative as in classical painting, but founded on the specific real-life motif. Many of his landscapes are symbolic. Suffice it to recall one of the most famous prints, *Red Fuji*, which even now is perceived as an embodiment of the spirit of Japan.

Admittedly, the majority of Hokusai's works are not pure landscapes: they stand rather on the dividing line between landscape and genre picture. This expresses itself not so much in the approach to composition as in the semantic stresses of the works. In Hokusai's prints the natural world comes across as an environment, a setting for the busy lives of people. The depiction of nature was not of intrinsic value, it was supposed to emphasize the significance of the real, everyday life of man.

The *Thirty-Six Views of Mount Fuji* series had a tremendous impact on contemporaries, including the thirty-year-old Ando Hiroshige, who until that time had not paid especial attention to the landscape. From the early 1830s he worked almost exclusively in that genre.

For his part, from the middle of that same decade, Hokusai, who was already over seventy, produced ever fewer landscape prints and devoted all his energy to the "historico-heroic" genre. Hiroshige became the leading exponent of the landscape print. In his works the characteristic features of *ukiyo-e* landscape were brought out in a more vivid and perfect manner.

Ando Hiroshige, quite possibly the most famous Japanese print artist beyond his native shores, was born in Edo in 1797. His father, Ando Genyemon, was a samurai serving in the fire brigade of the shogun, the military ruler of Japan. Hiroshige displayed a precocious talent for drawing as is demonstrated by a scroll, which he decorated at the age of ten. When the boy was only thirteen, his father died and he was obliged to take his place in the fire brigade, as the office was a hereditary one. Hiroshige, however, was possessed by the desire to become an artist. Two years later, he joined the pupils of one of the prominent print artists of the day, Utagawa Toyohiro. Originally Hiroshige had wanted to study under Toyokuni I (1765-1825), the head of the Utagawa School, but he was turned down. Toyohiro was not so well known as Toyokuni I, his fellow pupil in Utagawa Toyoharu's studio, but for Hiroshige he was surely the better teacher. Toyokuni was too strong an artistic personality. If he had worked side by side with him, Hiroshige's own original talent would, most likely, have been suppressed and there is no telling what would have become of him as an artist if he had followed the traditional course of the Utagawa School and specialized in theatrical prints and *bijin-ga*. Hiroshige did not spend long in Toyohiro's studio. After a year, in 1812, he was awarded a certificate acknowledging him as a qualified master of the Utagawa School. Hiroshige's early prints are derivative and of little interest. Produced in the *bijin-ga* and *yakusha-e* genres, they strongly betray the influence of the leading artists of the day: Toyokuni I, Hokusai and Eizan (1787-1867). After Toyohiro's death, Hiroshige was invited to take over his studio, but he rejected the idea – the traditional subject matter of the Utagawa School held little attraction for him. From the turn of the 1830s, all Hiroshige's thoughts were concentrated on the landscape and subsequently it became the chief theme of his creative work. Over the course of more than twenty years, the artist produced several series of prints, which demonstrated most vividly his talent in that sphere of art.

From the outset two main themes were evident in Hiroshige's landscape work: the Tokaido road and the sights of Edo (now Tokyo), the country's "Eastern Capital". Contemporaries looked on Hiroshige's works as reminders of visits to places noted for their beauty. The artist was quite often chided for distorting the true appearance of the locality depicted. It is difficult to discuss the reasons for such "inexactitude", but we do know that Hiroshige kept a travelling sketch book in which he recorded views that caught his attention, as was the case with the Tokaido road series, so it follows that all deviations from the real appearance were dictated by purely artistic considerations.

In the later series, *A Hundred Famous Views of Edo*, there are also quite a few prints that display that kind of approach to the "portrait" of a specific locality.

At the same time, Hiroshige not only depicted a locality, but also strove to convey its dominant emotion, the mood of nature. Possibly this second task was for him the primary one, which explains why he was capable of omitting or altering individual details, or even adding insignificant ones. Somewhat earlier such "distortions" can be found in Hiroshige's urban landscapes, the overwhelming majority of the views of Edo.

9. Aodo Denzen. 1748-1822
The Sensoji Monastery

10. Shiba Kokan. 1747-1818
View of the Mimeguri District
1783

Edo, then the capital of Japan, occupies a special place in both the life and work of Hiroshige. It was there that he was born, lived out his life, learned the painter's craft and made his name. He was formed as a landscape artist through observing nature and studying views of the city. The theme of the Eastern Capital was the natural leitmotif of his output.

Edo should not be imagined as a city in our modern understanding of the word. Densely built-up areas alternated with extensive rice paddies, parks and orchards. The overall effect was varied and picturesque. In all the series Hiroshige devoted to Edo we find not only urban views – streets, squares, bridges, but also pictures of rural nature – fields, the backwaters of rivers and waterfalls. The city landscapes are usually more precise from the topographical viewpoint than, say, the depictions of stations on the Tokaido road. That is not to state, however, that the emotional side of what he was conveying did not interest the artist here, rather that Hiroshige felt no need to resort to his own additions.

Thus it is the views of Edo which, to a greater extent than all the rest of the artist's output, demonstrate the distinctive features of that original phenomenon which we call "the Hiroshige landscape".

In the works devoted to the Eastern Capital, the artist sought to understand the spirit of nature, to convey its mood without deviating from the actual appearance of the city. If we reckon that the landscape is a portrait of a locality, then Hiroshige's landscape is its psychological portrait. Even the early landscape series, such as *Toto Meisho* (*Famous Views of the Eastern Capital*, 1831 and 1832-1835) and *Tokaido Gojusan Tsugi-No Uchi* (*Fifty-Three Stations on the Tokaido Road*, 1833-1834) clearly show the new element that Hiroshige introduced into *ukiyo-e* landscape that is not present in the work of its founder, Hokusai.

By the nature of his gift, Hokusai was least of all a contemplative artist. He was not content in his works to directly convey a motif from nature like his perspectivist predecessors; he stylized and abstracted the landscape, endowing it with a symbolic resonance. Quite frequently the depiction of nature takes second place to the search for a striking, masterfully constructed composition with a philosophical message. In other words, many of Hokusai's landscapes take the form of speculative ideas given visual embodiment on the basis of a combination of stylized elements drawn from the locality depicted.

In contrast to Hokusai, whose landscape bears the character of philosophical reflection on nature and man, Hiroshige is first and foremost a lyrical artist. In the landscape prints of the 1830s and 1840s, his response to nature was immediate and emotional. The main thing for him was to create such an image of nature that the viewer might sense its mood. Gentle lyricism, naturalness and simplicity were what marked Hiroshige's landscapes in that period.

In the 1850s Hiroshige's work underwent a radical change. Primarily this expressed itself in the ever more frequent use of the vertically-oriented portrait format, rather than the landscape format as before. Landscape and portrait formats are endowed with different expressive possibilities. The former suggests conveying a smooth, tranquil course of events. The latter, concealing within it the grain of "conflict", prompts the construction of a contrasting, tense, explosive composition. This can be easily seen by comparing Hiroshige's prints of the 1830s and 1840s with his late works: the *Hundred Famous Views of Edo*. In the series from the 1850s, such as *Rokuju Yoshu Meisho Zue* (*Famous Views of More Than Sixty Provinces*), the earlier smooth narrative manner has given way to abrupt compositional and chromatic contrasts. The depiction is at times eccentrically fragmented; sometimes dramatic intonations creep into the emotional atmosphere of the prints.

Various explanations have been given for this change in Hiroshige's style. Possibly it was connected with tragic events in his life. The 1830s were a time of success, calm creativity and domestic happiness. In 1839, though, the artist's wife died, followed in 1845 by his son Tojiro. It would be entirely natural that Hiroshige's spiritual state also reflected itself in his artistic vision of the world. There is, however, another possibility. By the 1850s we find Hiroshige a mature artist, the creator of many landscape series that have brought him fame. After the death of Hokusai, he was, moreover, the leading *ukiyo-e* landscape artist. But there was a negative side to that state of affairs. Hiroshige received many commissions and was forced to work quickly, at times carelessly. He began to entrust certain things to his pupils. Imitators with varying degrees of talent appeared.

Besides that, Hiroshige's own works of the 1840s added nothing new to what he had already achieved. Hiroshige seems to have grasped that the "lyrical landscape" theme that he had developed so successfully over almost two decades was exhausted. New paths needed to be sought. The painter's evolution led to an expansion of his artistic interpretation of the world. And in the series from the 1850s, the conveying of nature in its particular manifestations gave way to attempts to generalize from numerous observations of its life. This was not, however, analytical generalization, as seen with Hokusai, but rather emotional generalization: the main trend of Hiroshige's art remained the same.

Whatever the reasons, in the late 1840s, and particularly in the 1850s, new tendencies emerged in Hiroshige's work. They revealed themselves most clearly in the *Hundred Famous Views of Edo* series, which the artist himself considered his finest creation and which he intended as the final culmination of his career.

A Hundred Famous Views of Edo is the largest series of prints not only in Hiroshige's output, but also in the history of *ukiyo-e* as a whole. It actually consists of 118 different prints and was issued over an extended period by the Uoei publishing house under the direction of Uoya Eikichi. Publication lasted from 1856 to 1858 and the last prints were produced after the artist's death. Thirty-seven

prints appeared in 1856 (year 3 of the Ansei era, the Year of the Dragon), seventy-one in 1857 (year 4 of the Ansei era, the Year of the Snake) and ten in 1858 (year 5 of the Ansei era, the Year of the Horse). Not all of them were the work of Hiroshige himself – three were created after his death by his pupil Shigenobu (1826-1869) who assumed the pseudonym Hiroshige II.

The prints in the series were not issued in chronological order, but they were grouped according to the seasons: 42 prints relate to spring, 30 to summer, 26 to autumn and 20 to winter. We do not know whether this idea came from Hiroshige himself or was the publisher's initiative. To complete the series Uoya Eikichi issued one more print in which the others were listed in groups.

In the course of his almost thirty-year artistic career, Hiroshige addressed himself many times to the theme of Edo, and over the years developed a definite order for depicting localities in the Eastern Capital which he employed, at least partially, in the *Hundred Famous Views of Edo*. He invites the viewer to take a journey with him along the River Sumida, various views of which, Japanese scholars have calculated, appear in the artist's Edo series more often than any others. We accompany Hiroshige down the Sumida, pass under the Eitai bridge, cast a passing glance at Susaki, reach the mouth of the river in the Tsukuda-jima district, then, descending to the shore we pass the Shiba district and, climbing up the hill called Kasumigaseki, look back the way we have come. Although Hiroshige's last Edo series does go beyond the bounds of this route, as with the earlier sets it nonetheless remains the backbone of the "artistic tour of the Eastern Capital".

11. Ando Hiroshige
Cherry Tree in Blossom at Nakanomachi in Yoshiwara
From the series *The Sights of Edo*

12. Okumura Masanobu. 1686-1764
A large "perspective print" depicting all the stars of
the *Kabuki* theatre

13. Katsushika Hokusai. 1760-1849
The Poet Kakinomoto-no Hitomaro
From the series *The Anthology "A Hundred Poems
by a Hundred Poets" Explained by the Nurse*

14. Katsushika Hokusai. 1760-1849
Fisherman

Each print in *A Hundred Famous Views of Edo* includes texts presented in a standardized manner. The title of the series is given in cursive characters in a red or pink rectangle placed in the upper right-hand corner. Alongside, in a multicoloured square cartouche, is a brief, but adequate description of the locality depicted. One more red, less often yellow, rectangle is placed in the lower part of the print, to the left or right, occasionally in the centre. It is of the same size as that containing the title of the series. This is the artist's signature: Hiroshige ga ("Picture by Hiroshige") or Hiroshige hitsu ("Brush of Hiroshige"). At the bottom left, in the margin, we find the publisher's stamp: Shitaya Uoei ("Uoya Eikichi from the Shitaya district"). Alongside this stamp, or alternatively in the upper margin, are two censor's stamps: one simply stating "passed", the other giving the date in terms of the month and cyclical symbol of the year in which the print was produced.

It should be noted that, far from hindering the viewer's appreciation of the work, these colour cartouches were consciously incorporated into the decorative colour scheme and compositional structure. That is why, for example, Hiroshige did not adhere to one position for the rectangle containing his signature. If he needed to stress action developing along a diagonal, he placed the vivid red rectangular cartouches on that line. On the occasions when the composition is vertically oriented, the cartouches were placed on the same axis. This use of cartouches as chromatic and compositional accents in a print can be found earlier in Hiroshige's work, but only in this series is it so carefully thought-out and finely executed.

Colour accents not directly connected with the depiction intensify the decorative power of the prints in *A Hundred Famous Views of Edo*. This is a new quality that developed in Hiroshige's art only in the 1850s. The perception of many landscapes in the series as primarily decorative works is also encouraged by the bright variety of colours and, quite frequently, an unusual composition.

The compositional structure of the prints in *A Hundred Famous Views of Edo* is not entirely typical of Hiroshige's output. Among the prints of the series we find two main kinds of landscape: sketches directly from life and views in which decorative features are predominant.

The former are quite often landscapes depicted from a "natural" viewpoint. The gentle, lyrical mood reigning in these prints is suggestive of the works of the 1830s and at times they even look like fragments of larger horizontal compositions. Other "pure landscape" prints indicate a different approach. Here some single element – the prow of a boat, a flying crane, part of a temple roof – looms in the foreground and the landscape is shown in the distance across that object. This kind of composition is unusual for *ukiyo-e* landscapes. It is constructed in such a way as to make one feel present. The viewer enters the landscape, as it were, and the lower edge of the print becomes the point from which he observes what is taking place. Even when a composition is not enlivened by figures, the human presence can be clearly sensed; nature is depicted in the perception of someone viewing it. The depth of space is also conveyed through the juxtaposition of planes and accentuated at times by exaggerated linear perspective in the spirit of eighteenth-century *uki-e*. Probably the most successful prints of this kind, however, are *enkei* – "views from a distance" – in which the contrasting juxtaposition of planes is combined with an elevated viewpoint. Such landscapes justify their name: a boundless expanse opens up before the viewer's eyes; the landscape acquires a majestic resonance, dominated semantically and emotionally by the foreground depiction. Arguably the finest example of such a work is the famous print *Susaki and Jumantsubo in Fukagawa* in which an immense eagle in the foreground, shown from a dynamic, expressive angle against the background of a snow-covered stretch of seashore in the Fukagawa district, is perceived as the spirit of the elements raging above the desolate strand.

This compositional device is comprehended in an entirely different manner in the decorative prints, such as the celebrated *Irises in Horikiri* (*Horikiri-no hanashobu*). Here too, the foreground is brought as close as possible to the viewer, who peers, as it were, through the dense stand of flowers at the opposite bank, which is also covered with irises. The landscape as such plays no great role in the composition of this work, it acts only as a fairly neutral background. Effectively, the entire surface of the print is taken up with the depiction of the flowers, in the treatment of which naturalistic precision in the details is combined with the abstraction and subtle stylization of the whole. This approach to the depiction of flora is typical not so much of *ukiyo-e*, as of Japanese decorative painting, the Maruyama-Shijo and Rimpa Schools in particular, or indeed for works of applied art. It is hard to say which genre this print belongs to: the landscape or the *kacho-ga* ("painting of flowers and birds"), a field in which Hiroshige occasionally tried his hand.

While Hiroshige's prints of the 1830s and 1840s belong firmly to the landscape genre, many works in the *Hundred Famous Views of Edo* series cannot be attributed to any one specific genre. One of the finest examples of the mixing of genres is provided by *Rice Fields in the Asakusa District. Pilgrimage during the Torinomachi Festival* (*Asakusa-tanbo*

15. Katsushika Hokusai. 1760-1849
Fireworks at the Ryogokubashi Bridge
From the series *A New Set of Perspective Pictures*

16. Utagawa Toyoharu. 1735-1814
The Rebel An Lushan Attacking Emperor Hsuan Tsung
From the series *A New Set of Perspective Pictures. Ca.* 1770

17. Katsushika Hokusai. 1760-1849
View on a Fine, Breezy Day
From the series *Thirty-Six Views of Mount Fuji*
Mid 1820s-early 1830s

Torinomachi mairi). Through a window in the upper storey of a teahouse in the Yoshiwara district an extensive view opens of rice paddies and Mount Fuji in the distance. The landscape is black-and-white (only the roofs of the houses and Fujiyama are picked out in colour), while the procession of pilgrims heralded in the title is barely noticeable. A far more detailed working is given to the interior of the room from which the viewer looks out on the cold, wintry dawn. The room is empty, but a human presence can be clearly sensed. The cup and *tenugui* towel on the windowsill, the corner of a

roll of paper and the hairpins in a special case in the opposite corner of the print suggest that someone has just left the room. Besides, these details are themselves finely executed sketches, which one might term a still life, had such a genre existed in Japanese art.

As a matter of fact, it is to these elements that the greatest attention is devoted and they are what create the emotional atmosphere of the work.

The unusual angle of view here, as in other prints, helped the artist not simply to depict a particular locality, but also to convey the atmosphere, the human experience of the state of nature. The viewer becomes caught up in what is going on and perceives the scene depicted "from within". All the components of the composition are directed towards the creation of a definite psychological mood, which would facilitate the sensing of the state of nature. That was Hiroshige's main goal in *A Hundred Famous Views of Edo*, with the possible exception of the overtly decorative prints.

It is with that end in mind that the artist combined in the one-picture elements of various types of work: landscape, still life and genre painting. This approach is characteristic of many other prints in the series.

In *A Hundred Famous Views of Edo* Hiroshige arrived at an understanding, new for Japanese art, of the tasks to be fulfilled by the landscape, an understanding, which even Hokusai did not possess. Not merely the accurate depiction of a locality and not even the elevation of a specific topographic motif to the level of a symbol (as occurred occasionally in Hokusai's work), but the creation of an image of the natural world diffracted through the prism of human emotional perception, an image that would at the same time act on the viewer's psyche, creating a particular mood depending on the state of nature shown – that is the semantically many-sided, complex task that Hiroshige set himself. Such aims were new for the *ukiyo-e* landscape print, yet at the same time they accorded fully with its principles, to a far greater degree than the monumental landscapes of Hokusai, which are quite often divorced from human emotion and in which the human being comes across as an inanimate detail in the age-old constructions of nature.

In accordance with the *ukiyo-e* orientation on the everyday world, Hiroshige did not reject the commonplace. For him there were no "vulgar" objects and in his work any landscape motif reflected in human perception is a means of penetrating the essence of nature, its spirit.

Hiroshige's late landscapes are no less abstracted and symbolic than those of Hokusai.

In contrast to Hokusai, however, he does not break with one of the main principles of the greatest age of *ukiyo-e*: to convey not only what is taking place, but also its emotional atmosphere. Hiroshige's landscapes are not, of course, as monumental as those of Hokusai. They are more intimate, but at the same time considerably more complex and intense in emotional terms. Hiroshige's landscapes represented a new and final stage of development in the *ukiyo-e* landscape print and, more broadly, in the traditional art of Japan.

Spring

The choice of this particular print to open the series was most likely dictated by the fact that the Nihonbashi (the "Bridge of Japan") here functions as a symbol of Edo, the capital of Japan, and indeed of the country as a whole.

We are given a view into the distance that is dominated by two objects: the castle of the military ruler (*shogun*) surrounded by stylized belts of mist – a symbol of the ruling Tokugawa house, and Mount Fuji – a symbol of the country over which it ruled.

The Nihonbashi was one of the first bridges in the Eastern Capital. On the orders of Tokugawa Ieyasu, it was constructed across the river, which became known as Nihonbashigawa after the bridge (it connects the Sumidagawa river with the Sotobori canal) in the eighth year of Keicho (1603).

In the year following the construction of the bridge, 1604, Tokugawa Ieyasu issued a decree that assured the importance of the Nihonbashi for posterity: the middle of the bridge became the point from which all distances in the country were to be measured. Until very recently, a sign stating *Tokyo shi doro gempyo* – "the first milepost in Tokyo" – stood in the middle of the modern Nihonbashi, which was built in 1883. This was the starting point from the main highways that connected Edo with the rest of the country. There were five of these: the Tokaido and Nakasendo (part of which was known as the Kisokaido) which linked Edo and Kyoto by different routes; the Nikkokaido which led to Nikko, the site of Tokugawa Ieyasu's mausoleum; the Oshukaido, which headed into the north-east of the country as far as the province of Mutsu; and the Koshukaido which connected Edo with the city of Kofu.

The area around the Nihonbashi was one of the most important commercial centres in Edo. In Hiroshige's print the fishermen row their boats loaded with the night's catch, covered with matting, towards the northern bank. There, between two bridges, lay the largest fish-market in the Edo period, simply known as *Uogashi* – the "Fish Bank".

The market itself is depicted in full detail. The stalls, which extend in an unbroken line along the bank, are already open, offering fresh fish and all manner of seafood. It must be early: only merchants from other districts scurry between the stalls with baskets slung over their shoulders. After making their purchases, they head for all parts of the city.

The group of warehouses belonging to wholesale merchants covers the south bank of the Nihonbashigawa from this bridge to the following, Ichikobashi, visible in the background.

The Nihonbashi also functioned as the main centre for information in Edo. Here, on the square before the southern end of the bridge, was the largest site in Edo for public announcements (*kosatsuba*). Set up on the square, were a number (usually seven) of stands for tablets bearing announcements and decrees (*seisatsu*) very varied in content. The information was predominantly of a practical character: procedures for paying for horses hired at post stations; the rates for porters; and so on. There were also announcements of a deterrent nature: on the penalties for arson, forging coins, or selling bad-quality medicines. There were also bans of a more general sort, which by Hiroshige's time had lost their relevance, such as the prohibition of the Christian religion.

Such reminders were entirely appropriate here: close by the *kosatsuba* lay the execution ground where those guilty of the most heinous crimes – the murder of an overlord or a blood relative – were put to death by crucifixion. That was, however, quite a rare occurrence. More frequently punishment was meted out here to those discovered in adultery, to lovers who had attempted a suicide pact and monks who had offended against the vow of celibacy. Such "criminals" were "pilloried": tied up and made to sit on a piece of sacking.

After three days they were subjected to a "civil execution". The offenders were handed over to the headman of the *hinin* (literally "non-human") caste, a substratum of outcasts who, as far as the law was concerned, did not form part of the human community and were obliged to perform the dirtiest work. This, the most terrible place by the Nihonbashi for the Japanese, is also shown in Hiroshige's print: the *seisatsu* can be seen by the right-hand end of the bridge.

This is not, however, the main theme in Hiroshige's work. Life is in full swing around the Nihonbashi. The bridge that is the heart of the capital exudes an active, life-affirming atmosphere.

1. A Bright Morning after a Fall of Snow by the Nihonbashi Bridge

Nihonbashi Yukibare (5/1856)

This view of sailing boats against the background of dawn is the one obtained from the tall eminence called Kasumigasekizaka – the Hill of the Outpost of the Mists.

The locality was also known as Kasumigaseki. The origin of the name goes back into the distant past. According to legend, during his campaign against the Edzo, the wild tribes of eastern Japan, Yamato Takeru-no Mikoto was caught by a storm in the Sagami Bay and only survived through the self-sacrifice of his wife (see No. 31). When he reached dry land, Yamato Takeru climbed a hill so high that it seemed to enter the realm of clouds and fogs. The commander set up an advance post on the hill and called it the "Outpost of the Mists".

After Edo was made the capital, Tokugawa Ieyasu allocated Kasumigaseki for the residences of powerful members of the feudal hierarchy (*tozama-daimyo*) who included the influential princes Kurota Chikuzen-no kami and Asano, the latter being ruler of Aki (Hiroshima) province.

It is their mansions that are depicted to the right and left of the road. Asano's residence makes several appearances in the series (e.g. see No. 85), which in all probability is due to its association with the vengeance of the forty-seven *ronin* (samurai who had lost their overlord). This actual event from the beginning of the eighteenth century became the subject of a *Kabuki* play called *Chushingura* (*The Treasury of Samurai Loyalty*), which remains popular to the present day in Japan.

Only the boundary walls of the houses faced onto the street. The two-storey building on the right served as barracks for Kurota's samurai, while on the left the guard house (*tsujiban*) associated with Asano's mansion overlooks the street. The entrance to it is marked by two fairly small pines. The prevailing atmosphere on the street is one of merry-making. Hiroshige's depiction of the Outpost of the Mists is indeed set in a festive period, during the New Year celebrations. This is indicated by the pine at the gate (*kadomatsu*) in the right foreground.

A procession is advancing along the road, led by a man wearing formal clothing (*kariginu*) and a ceremonial hat (*kazetorieboshi*). He holds a pole topped by a bundle of paper strips attached in a particular fashion (*gohei*), which had a ritual meaning in Shintoism. Such a pole is called a *mando* ("10,000 times") and acts as a symbol of the Shintoist purification granted by a deity at the end of an act of worship addressed to it – or, more precisely, as a result of a ritual dance carried out by actors and paid for by donors. The man with the *mando* walks ahead of the actors who perform the *daikagura* ("music of the gods") as the ritualized Shintoist spectacles were originally called. With time such shows came to be put on by strolling players on the streets of Edo and elsewhere.

Their performances were like circus numbers, including juggling. Yet the original "lion dance" (*shishimai*), performed at the Ise shrine, was not forgotten (indeed, it remained the high-point of the performance), just as the general religious mood of the performance was preserved: the board attached to the *mando* below the *gohei* usually bore the name of Amaterasu, the goddess of the sun and supreme deity of the Shintoist pantheon to whom Ise-jingu, the chief Shintoist shrine in Japan, is dedicated.

The actors went from house to house, performing songs and dances intended to invoke blessings.

During the New Year festivities roughly the same thing was done by two actors who presented the *manzai* ("10,000 years of life"), a dance wishing the audience longevity. They are depicted to the left of the *daikagura* procession. In the first days of the New Year they performed songs and dances for a fee in people's homes, wishing them long life and happiness.

To the left, a servant hurries from a shop selling rice cakes and raw fish (*sushi*). He carries on his shoulder the boxes of orders that have to be delivered to customers. Climbing the slope behind the *daikagura* procession is a detachment of samurai returning from the shogun's castle after officially paying their respects.

2. The Outpost of the Mists

Kasumigaseki (1/1857)

This print depicts one of the most aristocratic areas of the Eastern Capital – the place known as Hibiya in the Soto-Sakurada district.

At the time when the capital was moved to Edo, Hibiya was a small fishing village and for many years afterwards there were quite a number of stalls here trading in freshly-caught fish and other seafood.

After Ieyasu came to Edo, a considerable portion of Soto-Sakurada was occupied by the mansions of major feudal lords. In particular, the estate of the powerful Nabeshima clan, the rulers of the province of Saga, was located there.

Hiroshige places us directly opposite this estate and the red gates of the house are the first thing to catch our attention. The artist has depicted the façade of the estate, running along the ditch, which connects the Sotobori and Uchibori canals with an almost documentary precision. This is reckoned to be the most detailed image of a *daimyo* estate in *ukiyo-e* art.

The building which functions as a sort of symbol for the life lived by the highest, ruling class is not only shown from the lower city, from the Yamashitacho quarter, which was inhabited by merchants and craftsmen, and noted as a place for diversions of various kinds, but also viewed "through the eyes" of the ordinary citizens.

Although they are not actually there, two people are invisibly present in the foreground. They are playing at shuttlecock. Left and right are two painted battledores (properly *hagoita*) used in the game. The shuttlecock itself hangs frozen in the air. Two further details also catch the attention: the traditional and most common New Year decoration (*kadomatsu*), a decorated pine in front of the entrance in the foreground, and the kites fluttering in the sky. These are indisputable signs that the start of the New Year is depicted here.

Kite flying was a favourite amusement for children. In Edo, the fun began on the 15th and 16th days of the First Month. Everybody flew kites, at the *daimyo* mansions and in the lower-class districts. They decorated them with depictions of famous generals, armed warriors or characters, typically of a "threatening" nature: "storm", "wind", "thunder" and the like. The general preference, nonetheless, was for martial subjects, since kite fights were very much in fashion. This can be seen in Hiroshige's print too: the kite flying in the foreground is victorious. Its less fortunate opponent is hanging on someone else's kite-string in the depths of the picture.

The main symbols of the New Year here are, however, the *hagoita*. In Edo it became the custom to mark the first day of the New Year with a game of shuttlecock, which began around noon.

3. Hibiya in the Soto-Sakurada District, Seen from the Yamashita Quarter

Yamashitacho Hibiya Soto-Sakurada (12/1857)

Here we are given a view from the mouth of the Sumidagawa (at this point it is known as the Okawa), where the river enters Edo Bay, towards Tsukudajima Island. The viewer is placed, as it were, in a boat passing beneath the Eitaibashi Bridge, one of the piers of which frames the picture on the left.

Eitaibashi is the largest bridge and one of the oldest across the Sumidagawa. It was constructed in the 11th year of Genroku (1698) on the site of a ferry. The story goes that it was built from materials left over after the construction of the Kanyeiji Monastery on Ueno Hill (see No. 11). The bridge stands almost at the mouth of the Sumidagawa, which sea-going ships could enter because the piers of the bridge were unusually high. To the west of the Eitaibashi rose Mount Fuji, to the north Mount Tsukuba, to the south lay the place called Hikone, to the east the countryside of Kazusa province. The panorama from the bridge developed into one of the traditional themes of Japanese poetry in the Edo period.

The bridge was, however, frequently damaged by floods and had to be repaired at considerable expense. Finally, the government decided to give up the struggle and abandon the Eitaibashi. At that point the people living near the bridge applied to the city council with a request to be allowed to pay for the upkeep of the bridge themselves. Permission was granted and they were allowed to compensate their losses by charging each person who crossed the bridge. Samurai were, incidentally, exempted from the toll, as were Buddhist monks and Shinto priests.

On the prow of the boat, poking out from behind the pier of the bridge behind which unfolds a view of a bay, a brazier is burning. In this area it was usual to go out at night for the *shirauo*, a small transparent fish which turns milky white when cooked. The *shirauo* caught by the local fishermen was supplied to the shogun's court.

The beginnings of this industry were already laid by Tokugawa Ieyasu who issued a special decree obliging fishermen who specialized in catching *shirauo* to move from Setsu (in Osaka Prefecture) to the new capital. The fishermen's duties included keeping a watch on nocturnal activities in Edo Bay, the approach to the capital from the sea.

The fires which were lit in special metal braziers hanging from the prows of the boats became one of the main distinctive signs of this area, particularly in the *shirauo* season – between the 11th and 3rd months inclusive.

In the distance, beyond the large cargo vessels riding at anchor we can see Mount Tsukuda (see No. 55), the location of the village which was home to the *shirauo* fishermen.

The view of Tsukudajima cannot be described as particularly interesting in compositional terms, but its undeniable virtues must include the way in which it conveys nightime illumination: the moon, stars and braziers create a glittering, shifting half-light which is also described in Kawatake Mokuami's work *Shiranami gonin otoko* (*Five Robbers*, 1816–1893). The play, put on in the *Kabuki* theatre four years after the publication of Hiroshige's series, contains this passage:

In the spring twilights
The moon too is pale.
And the fires on the boats using light to catch *shirauo*
Are tugged about by the foggy shroud.

4. Tsukudajima Island from the Eitaibashi Bridge

Eitaibashi Tsukudajima (2/1857)

The white summit of Mount Fuji rises from a scarlet strip of dawn sky. The even line of houses belonging to common people that forms the background of the print is disrupted only by the slight curve of the bridge built across the Yagenbori canal at the point where it joins the Sumidagawa.

This bridge is known as Moto-Yanagibashi - the "True Willow Bridge". When a new bridge was constructed across the Kandagawa in 1693 and also given the name Yanagibashi, or "Willow Bridge", the older Yanagibashi came to be prefixed "Moto" - "True, Genuine".

At this early hour boats are passing along the Sumidagawa loaded with goods for the numerous markets that open while it is still dark. A sharply dissonant contrast to the measured fluidity of the composition erupts in the form of the Drum Tower (*kuro*) depicted in the foreground. It stands in the Ekoin area, which belongs to a Buddhist monastery of the Jodo (Pure Earth) school. Ekoin was noted, among other things, for the *sumo* wrestling contests that were held here twice a year.

Many features of the monastery are connected with this sport which has ritual origins. There is, for example, the Chikarazuka ("Tumulus of Strength"), which incorporates religious offerings: knots of hair from the heads of champion wrestlers and parts of their mortal remains. To this day, the Chikarazuka is revered by *sumo* wrestlers as a sacred place.

The Drum Tower is also connected with *sumo* matches. The red coloured drum itself can be seen in the upper right-hand part of the print. It was used to announce the start of a contest, while the poles with pieces of cloth dangling from them (*bonten*) indicated that the weather was favourable and that the contest would take place.

The history of this monastery was far from untroubled. Its very appearance was the result of a tremendous disaster - the great fire of 1657, which became known as Nagasode ("Long sleeves"). The conflagration raged for two days and took the lives of over 108,000 people. It was on the shogun's orders, for the burial of those who had no relatives capable of performing the funeral rites, that Ekoin was constructed. The name if translated means "the Temple of Funeral Rites". It also has an official title - Muenji ("the Monastery of those without Kin"). Soon grave memorials were being raised here to the victims of other natural disasters, and also for animals who had no one to pray for them.

With time, Ekoin distinguished itself as a monastery in which animals, primarily dogs and cats, were accorded special attention. This lay within the bounds of the Biddhist world-view: animals were considered unfortunate reincarnations of souls which once possessed human forms and might in their next lives again enter the world as people.

The monastery had a special link with cats. Legend has it that a family called Tomita lived in Nihonbashi. The head of the family found himself threatened with complete ruin. The situation was saved by the family cat. One day it returned home with a gold coin in its mouth, which proved sufficient for its master to settle his affairs. When the cat died, he buried it at Ekoin and put up a monument to it. This grave is known as Nekozuka ("the Cat's Tumulus") and can still be seen today. When the story became public knowledge other owners began to bury their beloved pets at Ekoin.

The most important memorial of the monastery is the Mizuko-zaka ("Grave of the Child in the Waters") commissioned by Matsudaira Sadanobu (1758-1829) and erected in 1793. It is dedicated to the memory of unborn children and those who died at birth.

5. The Ekoin Monastery at Ryogoku and the Moto-Yanagibashi Bridge

Ryogoku Ekoin. Motoyanagibashi (5/1857)

When Hiroshige takes us to the Hatsune-no baba racetrack, we find ourselves in one of the quietest places in the Eastern Capital. On the South-West it extends as far as the Asakusa-gomon gate, on the north its boundary is Third Street. In the early Edo period this spot, like the whole of the Bakurocho quarter, was the scene of lively horse-dealing. The name of the quarter, which today means "The Feeding of Horses" was originally written with different characters, although the pronounciation was the same. At first it meant "Horse-Trader" and referred to a certain Takagi Gembei, who in the early Edo years organized a regular horse fair here. The horses were brought to the capital along the Oshukaido highway, which linked it to the northern provinces. The same route was taken by traders, travellers and state officials, including the *gundai*, who were responsible for collecting taxes in the lands ruled directly by the shogun. The official residence of the *gundai* stood in Bakurocho by the Asakusa-gomon gate. There was always a large number of visiting provincials in this institution and soon quite a few inns and hostelries appeared here. The roofs of buildings visible in the middle ground of the print represent that small district.

Breaking with his usual habit, Hiroshige has depicted a fire tower in every detail close to the foreground of the print. He even includes the bell used as a fire alarm.

In front of the area of hostelries lay the Hatsune-no baba racetrack, the oldest in Edo. The site was directly connected with the Battle of Sekigahara in 1600 that brought the Tokugawa house to power.

It was here at Hatsune-no baba, on the eve of the battle, that horses were selected for Tokugawa Ieyasu's army.

As the years went by, the racetrack was used less and less to train the samurai of the shogun's army to ride and to hone their equestrian skills. It was not built over, however, and became slowly overgrown with grass in its enclosure of willows.

With time the character of the place changed. Together with Bakurocho, it became a centre for working and selling fabrics. Only a few dozen yards from Hatsune-no baba lay the Konyacho quarter (see No. 75), where the houses and workshops of the cloth-dyers were. They made use of the abandoned racetrack, covering it with tall poles on which they hung the finished cloth to dry.

6. The Hatsune-no baba Racetrack in the Bakurocho Quarter

Bakurocho Hatsune-no baba (9/1857)

Momendana is an alternative appellation for First Street in the Odemmacho quarter. This quarter was formed at the very start of the Edo period. Its name means "The Great Post Station". It was located in the immediate vicinity of the Nihonbashi, the starting point for journeys from the Eastern Capital.

From the second half of the seventeenth century, merchants trading in fabrics began to concentrate their businesses in this quarter. Large wholesale shops were located on First Street. There were about fifty of these, forming an unbroken row on either side of the street.

Hiroshige shows us First Street from the gate, which closed off the quarter. From the moment the new capital was founded, gates like these were installed in all the quarters of Edo for crime prevention and, most importantly, fire prevention. At night the gates were closed and a team of fire fighters drawn by *rota* from the citizens of the quarter began its duty watch.

The section of the street depicted in this print contained three shops: Tabataya, Masuya and, further back, Shimaya. They are all in line and their façades are completely identical. This was not mere whim, but a requirement of the city authorities. The shops can be told apart only by signs, or more precisely curtains (*noren*) bearing the name and trade mark of the business and by a low wall rising above the level of the roof (*neribeya*). Apart from this wall, each shop had on its roof baskets of vessels containing rainwater as a measure against fire.

In the foreground two geishas accompanied by a servant-girl are walking for the gate. Their slightly disordered clothing and somewhat unsteady gait indicate that it has been an entertaining evening.

7. The Street of Fabric Shops in the Odemmacho Quarter

Odemmacho momendana (4/1858)

A street straight as an arrow runs right to the very foot of Mount Fuji, which is depicted in the centre of the print. The mountain is separated from the cityscape by a strip of stylized clouds that Hiroshige "borrowed" from the repertoire of classical painting: Fuji seems to exist in a different world. It reigns above the urban bustle of the commercial quarter near the Nihonbashi (see No. 1) without coming into contact with it. The Surugacho quarter lay on either side of the street, which Hiroshige depicted.

The view of Fuji from Surugacho was one of the sights of Edo. Less "loftily", the quarter was noted for its cloth shops, which belonged to the Mitsui family and were called Echigoya. There were so many of them here that Echigoya became an alternative name for the whole quarter.

These same shops feature in Hiroshige's print. The name and Echigoya trade mark feature on the awnings (*noren*) of buildings on both sides of the street which disappears beyond the horizon – its far end is lost in the strips of cloud. The Echigoya trade mark consisted of a circle containing two symbols: *mitsu* meaning "three" and *i* meaning "well", which between them made up the surname of the owners. The business was founded by Mitsui Hachiroemon Takatoshi, a native of Ise province. Takatoshi came to the capital while still a child, serving first in his elder brother's fabric shop, before opening his own in the Hommachi quarter of the Nihonbashi district in the year 1673.

His business flourished, in no small part due to the fact the way in which he traded. Echigoya was the first place in Japan to introduce non-negotiable prices and payment in cash (*genkin-kakenashi*). Usually commodities of any sort of size were obtained on credit; the two parties haggled over the price, which was therefore pitched high to start with.

The frequent fires that afflicted Hommachi obliged Mitsui to move his business elsewhere. Echigoya began operating in Surugacho, where it can still be found today, having become part of the immense financial and commercial empire called Mitsui-Mitsukoshi. On the left of his print Hiroshige depicted a shop dealing in silks.

The strictly symmetrical composition in this print strikes a discordant note with the other works of the series. This approach was, however, traditional and dictated by the subject itself. The use of exaggerated perspective when depicting distant vistas was common among the creators of "perspective prints" in the face of similar artistic tasks.

8. The Surugacho Quarter

Surugacho (9/1856)

In the thirteenth year of Kanyei (1636) the Sujikai-gomon gate was constructed on the road leading from the Nihonbashi bridge (see No. 1) to Ueno (see No. 11) for the inspection of travellers. Somewhat earlier a bridge with the same name (the Sujikaibashi) was constructed across the Kandagawa river.

The artist places his viewer beneath the gate, looking out on the open space known as *hirokoji*, which was intended to serve as a sort of fire-break. This square was also by way of being a major road junction.

A large number of minor roads led off the square. The people of Edo were quite justified in dubbing the place Yatsukoji – "Eight Streets". In point of fact there were at least ten roads running off the Yatsukoji.

Standing in the more distant part of the square, next to a *daimyo*'s mansion, is a small guardhouse, which Hiroshige depicted in the upper left-hand part of the print. Quite possibly this mansion is the destination of a procession consisting of several palanquins (*kago*), servants carrying luggage baskets and samurai guards. The procession is led by "maids of honour" who serve at the court of an influential prince. The palanquin with a red cloth roof in all probability contains the *daimyo*'s spouse.

On the Yatsukoji did not remain completely empty. Like other *hirokoji* it was built upon. Temporary structures were put up here, such as the tea stall that Hiroshige depicted in the lower right-hand corner.

On the other side of the Kandagawa we can see the majestic buildings of the Kanda-myojin, one of the most popular Shinto holy places among those born and bred in the city. In this print Hiroshige depicted the shrine, and, most notably, its main building from the outside, as if inviting the viewer to move on to the next print, which shows the precincts.

9. Yatsukoji Square Seen from the Sujikai Gate

Sujikai-uchi Yatsukoji (11/1857)

This print takes the viewer onto the grounds of the Kanda-myojin shrine. On the right-hand side the corner of the main building in the complex (the *honden*) is visible.

The tall hill on which the Kanda shrine is located provides a view far out over the city with its countless single-storey grey houses. Day is about to break and three servants of the Kanda-myojin have gathered to watch the sunrise on the terrace occupied by a tea shop. Standing on the left is a Shinto priest (*kannushi*), already dressed in his ceremonial robes; on the right is a priestess (*miko*) whose duties include the performance of ritual dances (*kagura*) and soothsaying; the third figure is a servant carrying a wooden tub.

Kanda-myojin was noted for the views to be had from its terrace. The shrine was also one of the most ancient in Edo. It had been founded in the year 730 in the village of Shibasaki (the present-day Otemachi quarter). In 1603 it was moved to the Surugadai hill, and shifted again in 1615 to its present site. At that last date, the shogun granted the Kanda shrine an immense tract of land. Its "parish" included all the inhabitants of the Kanda district and of many quarters in the Nihonbashi district.

Kanda-myojin owed its popularity on an "official" level to the story that it had been the place where in 1600 Ieyasu prayed for victory before the Battle of Sekigahara, which decided the fate of the whole country.

Kanda-myojin is dedicated to two Shintoist deities – Okuninushi-no mikoto and Sukunahikona-no mikoto. It was to Okuni-nushi, the divine peacemaker who put an end to internal strife, that Ieyasu prayed. One further figure is venerated at the shrine: the deified Taira-no Masakado (?-940), a rebel from the mid-Heian period who aspired to seize the imperial throne but was defeated by the no-less-legendary warrior Fujiwara Hidesato. At Otemachi there was also the tumulus raised over the grave where Masakado's decapitated head was buried.

Tales endowed Masakado with powers of sorcery: he is supposed, for example, to have made several magical likenesses of himself in order to avoid assassination. In popular belief, however, he came to be venerated as a bringer of well-being.

In general the shrine was held to be the dwelling-place of the spirits who guarded the capital. Perhaps for that reason the Kanda-matsuri temple festival was the most popular holiday among the natives of the city.

Only one shrine in the Eastern Capital could compete with it – the Hie Sanno-jinja (see No. 51). The city authorities ordered that their temple festivals, Sanno-matsuri and Kanda-matsuri, be observed alternately, one one year, one the next. They were too costly and contradicted the government's ordinances regarding economy in all spheres of life.

The Sanno-matsuri and especially the Kanda-matsuri were noted for their inordinate opulence. Both were special festivals since they were presented for the viewing of the shogun and his courtiers.

The procession, which consisted of 36 decorative floats (*sansha*) drawn by oxen and an immense number of palanquins (*o-mikoshi*), passed through the Tayasu-mon gate, paraded in front of the shogun and left the castle through the Takebashi-mon gate. In the Edo period, the festival was held on the 15th day of the Ninth Month, the day of the Battle of Sekigahara. The victory in that encounter was granted to Ieyasu in accordance with his prayer at Kanda-myojin, and the honorific title "victory-bringing" (*kachimamori*) was therefore added to its name.

This chain of associations would have arisen inevitably and naturally in the minds of Hiroshige's contemporaries. The print, though, depicts something different – the quiet start to a day of noise and bustle, which they all were in the Eastern Capital's most frequently visited holy place.

10. The Kanda-myojin Shrine at Daybreak

Kanda-myojin akebono-no kei (9/1857)

Kiyomizudo was the most important of the temples of the Kanyeiji monastery, one of the main Buddhist centres in the Eastern Capital. While Zojoji (see No. 99) was a sort of focal point for Buddhist learning, a theological institute in the Tokugawa era, Kanyeiji acted as a symbol for the established status of Buddhism in the state during the Edo period. It is no coincidence that the burials of the ruling family were "divided" between these two monasteries: six mausoleums of Tokugawa shoguns were at Zojoji, another six in the cemetery at Kanyeiji. The monastery is situated at a place called Ueno. Literally translated this means "upper field".

According to one of the many versions, this hill in the central part of the city acquired the name Ueno in the late sixteenth - early seventeenth century, after the *daimyo* Todo Takatora (1556-1630), famous as the builder of Edo Castle, constructed his own mansion here.

The monastery owed its appearance to a monk named Nankobo Tenkai (1536-1643). Tenkai, who distinguished himself both as a statesman and as a theologian, was arguably the brightest figure in Japanese Buddhism during the Tokugawa period. One of the closest advisors of Ieyasu and his two immediate successors, Tenkai was privately referred to as "a minister in priestly vestments" (*kokue-no saisho*). He also masterminded a tremendous bibliographic undertaking - the publication of the Tripitaka (Daizokyo), the many-volume Buddhist canon. The time of building gave the monastery its name - Kanyeiji means "the monastery of the Kaneyi years".

The choice of location for the monastery was a carefully considered one. Tenkai belonged to the Tendai school, whose main monastery, Enryakuji, was on the hill called Hieizan in Kyoto. The terrain at Ueno was similar to that around Enryakuji and Kanyeiji was constructed in imitation of the older monastery. In both cases they derived their names from the era (Enryaku and Kanyei) in which they were built. The Kyoto stronghold of the Tendai school was created in the ninth century as a mystic defence for the capital (then known as Heian) from evil spirits. According to Chinese beliefs, such spirits were located to the north-east and Enryakuji stood to the north-east of the Emperor's palace. Kanyeiji, in turn, was raised to the north-east of the shogun's castle in order to protect it from fires and other misfortunes. At the same time as the main building, other structures were put up in the monastery: the Hokkedo ("Temple of the Flower of the Law"),

a repository for sutras, the Niomon gate and the Toshogu, Ieyasu's mausoleum.

Somewhat later other buildings were completed: a five-tier pagoda, the pavilion of the Great Buddha and also the Kiyomizu-do temple and a bell-tower which served as a kind of clock tower. Later, following Ieyasu's instructions, such towers were erected in every district of the new capital. Their bells rang the hours, or to be more precise, the watches, of which there were twelve in a 24-hour period. At first every successive watch was announced by three strikes of the bell; later the number corresponded to that of the watch.

But none of the bells in the capital could compete with those of Kanyeiji, with the possible exception of the Zojoji bells at Asakusa. Comparing the tones of Ueno and Asakusa was a favourite everyday pastime for the citizens of Edo. This tradition is certainly reflected in a poem by the famous poet Matsuo Basho (1644-1694): In the clouds of springtime flowers / It is not clear: does the sound of the bell / Come from Ueno or from Asakusa?

Within the main temple a statue of the Thousand-Armed Kannon was set up which had been sent to Tenkai by the abbot of Kiyomizu-dera in Kyoto. The Thousand-Armed Kannon, a bodhisattva of kindness and compassion, has a "special function" at Kanyeiji monastery - that of bringing offspring. In the temple precincts today, just as in Hiroshige's time, the visitor will see a countless host of dolls, votive offerings made by couples whose prayers have been answered.

In the print Hiroshige has placed the red terrace wreathed in the cherry blossom of spring in the foreground. From it, there is a view of the Shinobazu-no ike - a pond, whose name has a touch of humour about it. The hill, at the base of which it lies, had in ancient times been known as Shinobu-ga oka - "Hill of Patience". The pond, in all likelihood, was notable for its diametrically opposite character, and was accordingly given a negative form of the same name - "Impatient Pond". Tenkai transformed this body of fresh water that was once part of Edo Bay, again drawing on familiar topography. The monk fancied a resemblance between this pond and the celebrated Lake Biwa, close to the old capital. In order to increase the similarity, Tenkai ordered the creation of an artificial island in the pond in imitation of Chikubujima, the island in Lake Biwa. The island is linked to the shore by a causeway and a bridge leading to the temple of Benzaiten, one of the seven gods of happiness.

In Hiroshige's print the presence of the island and the temple are only hinted at: the narrow strip of land leading to them from the path in front of the Kiyomizudo seems to simply stick out into the pond.

The complex, which Tenkai created, can be regarded as a reduced-size copy of the ancient temples of Kyoto. For contemporary Edoans, however, Kanyeiji was a peak of perfection before which the whole of classical antiquity paled. A *senryu* (seventeen-syllable humorous poem) composed on the completion of the monastery after some eighty years of construction was often quoted among the citizens: Kanyeiji! / Ancient temples gleaming gold and silver / Are nought compared to this!

The poem reflected the attitude of Edo's populace to the monastery at Ueno: there was nothing better; it was more beautiful even than Kyoto's Kinkakuji and Ginkakuji (Gold and Silver Pavilions) which even now are one of the chief exotic sights of Kyoto.

Hiroshige depicted Kiyomizudo in spring, when it is literally swimming in white cherry blossom. The choice of season was quite deliberate. The cherry-trees, which had already been planted by the third shogun, Iemitsu, were a local prodigy and brought Ueno fame as the best place for the admiration of the spring blossom (*hanami*). The hanami was accompanied by a banquet, and no few of the admirers were merry with drink. This too found reflection in poetry.

For example, the poetess O-Aki, a pupil of the celebrated Muroi Kikaku (1661-1707) composed an ad-lib verse at the age of thirteen, when she attended the blossom festival at Ueno: The cherry tree is leaning / Dangerously by the well. / Obviously it too is drunk on the wine.

This subtle piece of observation cast in poetry brought O-Aki fame. The citizens immediately responded, though, with their own *senryu*: The cherry tree at the edge of the well / Made a name / For O-Aki.

Ueno was also noted for its pines, or at least for one of them - the Tsuki-no matsu, "Moon Pine", depicted in the left-hand part of the print. The unusual shape of one branch, forming a regular circle, fascinated the Edoans. They liked to view the moon through it as it formed an excellent sort of frame. Hiroshige shared this affection.

The Moon Pine appears twice in our series. The second time it is the chief protagonist of a separate work (see No. 89).

11. The Kiyomizudo Temple and Shinobazu Pond at Ueno

Ueno Kiyomizudo Shinobazu-no ike (4/1856)

Yamashita, literally "Below the Hill", was an area of wasteland at the foot of Ueno hill. It was supposed to serve as a fire-break, since flames could easily jump across from one wooden building to another. This open area was deliberately created in 1737. In overpopulated Edo empty spaces were at a very high premium. Soon various eating-houses, wine-shops and restaurants appeared here (one of which is depicted on the right-hand side of the engraving). The sign, with a trademark in the centre, proclaims it to be the Iseya and also indicates the speciality of the house: rice (*shisomeshi*) flavoured with a herb (*shiso*) that gives a minty taste. Lower down the hill, directly beneath the Iseya, stands a fishmonger's with all manner of seafood on display. In particular we can make out two huge skates hanging from the roof.

Yamashita was famous for street performances, including acrobats, tightrope-walkers, dancers, magicians and *hoka* – figures dressed up as monks with a characteristic bamboo ornament behind their backs who performed dances and songs to the accompaniment of the yatsuhachi, a small drum attached to the chest.

The rather low class local courtesans were customarily referred to as *kekoro* – "sluts". By the time this series was published, the fame of the *kekoro* had faded somewhat, but even in the middle of the nineteenth century they remained a distinctive feature of Yamashita.

The many shops in Yamashita sold just about everything: paper, brocade, medicines, oil, dried fish, tea, confectionery and candles. The Edoans often called these establishments "the shops of the Buddha" (*hotokedana*), possibly because they were in the immediate vicinity of Kanyeiji (see No. 11). The Iseya touches the southern edge of the monastery grounds and the stone wall running to the left from the centre of the print leads to the monastery.

The place depicted in this print is immediately adjacent to the Mihashi, the "Three Bridges" across the little Shinobugawa river which flows into the Shinobazu-no ike pond. Originally there was only one bridge here, leading to the burial place of the shoguns constructed in the Kanyeiji monastery in 1623. It became a part of the ceremonial route taken by rulers when visiting the graves of their precursors. However, due to the widening of a number of streets near the Shinobugawa after the great fire of 1657, two more bridges were constructed and the name Mihashi arose. Tradition attributed particular functions to each of the bridges. The central one was reserved exclusively for the shogun's procession; the other two were used by ordinary pedestrians. The eastern bridge was also the one across which bound criminals were conducted, while the western one was prescribed for funeral processions.

The group of women beneath parasols is heading for one of those bridges. They are probably "maids of honour" from the mansion of one of the *daimyo* making for Kanyeiji in order to pay homage at the graves of the ancestors of the ruling shogun.

The white and pink stylized clouds (*suyarigasumi*) in the centre of the print are another reminder of Kanyeiji. The monastery with its blossoming cherry-trees should be located beneath these clouds and their white and pink mist, as the American researcher Henry D. Smith II acutely observed, is perceived as the "reflection" of those magnificent flowers. Directly beneath the *suyarigasumi*, surrounded by trees lower down the slope stands a fairly small structure heralded by a torii gate. This is Gojo-tenjin, a Shinto shrine dedicated to Sugawara-no Mitizane (845-903), a minister and poet, the deified patron of scholars and students.

The authorship of the present print is open to question, since it is one of the three (see Nos. 41 and 114), which were issued in the Tenth Month of 1858, that is to say a month after Hiroshige's death. The opinion has become fairly firmly established among scholars that it was created by Shigenobu (Hiroshige II), a pupil of Hiroshige I. There are, however, other views. The most correct would seem to be that Hiroshige (who died suddenly in an epidemic) himself prepared the sketches, but his pupil worked them up.

12. Yamashita at Ueno

Ueno Yamashita (10/1858)

Ueno hill crowned by the Kanyeiji monastery (see No. 11) was one of the main centres of attraction in the Eastern Capital. Hiroshige depicted it several times from different angles.

The word Shitaya ("Lower Valley") was used to describe a fairly extensive area at the foot of Ueno Hill. The street here was part of the ceremonial route used by the shogun when visiting the graves of his predecessors in Kanyeiji. In the depths of the print we can make out the dark walls of the monastery complex.

Open spaces never remained empty for long in the overcrowded capital. The whole length of Shitaya's *hirokoji* was soon occupied by stalls, eating-places and shops. The sign of the shop in the foreground selling silk fabrics announces that it belongs to Ito Matsuzakaya. Today the business has become one of Tokyo's major department stores.

Here, as in the vicinity of the Three Bridges across the Shinobugawa, the street is exceptionally busy. A group of women carrying parasols is making its way up the middle. The women are dressed in a variety of costumes and behave in an easy manner. Most probably they are servants on a trip to admire the cherry blossoms at Kanyeiji. They are followed by porters carrying a box of refreshments.

This procession is approaching a small building with red badges on its windows, which stands somewhat forward of the building line. This is a hairdresser's, an institution which played an important role in city life,

among other things as a source of information about fashions. The depiction of something on the awnings (*noren*) of Edo's hairdressers' was a sure sign that it was in vogue, in the theatre, art or daily life.

The women are followed by three samurai, each with the two swords in his belt that only representatives of the military class could wear in the Edo period. One element of their appearance is quite striking – the long, loose trousers.

A Hundred Famous Views of Edo was published in the late 1850s. Several years had already passed since the visits made in 1853-1854 by the squadrons of the American Commodore Matthew Perry (1794-1858) and the Russian Count Yefim Putiatin (1804-1883), which effectively "opened up" Japan. Europeans had become an increasingly common sight on the streets of Japanese cities and their clothing came into fashion among the progressively-minded youth. This explains the extravagant dress of these samurai, combining the traditional kimono with European-style trousers. This trend began in the late 1850s and became almost the norm by the next decade, the start of the Meiji period (1868-1912) which saw the rapid penetration of Western culture into all spheres of Japanese life. The early years were marked by a chaotic, sometimes amusing fusion of two mindsets: sometimes it is referred to as "the period of the kimono and the bowler hat". The traditional coexisted paradoxically with the new, in dress as in life as a whole.

13. Hirokoji Street in the Shitaya District

Shitaya hirokoji (9/1856)

Nippori was part of one of the quietest areas of the Eastern Capital, lying between Ueno and another hill. The name means "the village of life, day in, day out", suggesting a calm, unhurried existence.

Until the 1670s and 1680s, there was nothing remarkable about the place, but then several existing monasteries and Shinto shrines moved here and new ones were constructed. The most notable were Myoryuji, Shushoin and Shounji. All three monasteries were famous for their gardens.

Hiroshige takes us to the Shushoin monastery belonging to the Nichiren school, which was founded in 1575 and moved to Nippori in 1668. The gardens were created in imitation of those of Myoryuji, but were distinctively adorned by artificial hills and rocks of eccentric shape and interesting examples of topiary. One tree trimmed to look like a sailing boat can be seen on the right of Hiroshige's print.

(Henry D. Smith II was the first to point this out.) In the depths of the print we see the gate marking the road to Suwa-jinja (see No. 15), a Shinto shrine located on the monastery grounds. To the left of the gate are the roofs of the Banjinsha shrine, dedicated to the guardian-deities who protected the sacred Buddhist scriptures in turn throughout the year.

The Shushoin monastery was a favourite place of relaxation among the inhabitants of Edo. Kikuoka Senryo's work Edo sunago ("Edo Gilding"), published in 1732, states: "As at Myoryuji, the gardens of this monastery are interesting. There are, moreover, many tea pavilions, which have been constructed so as to provide a fine view. And how can I describe how beautiful they are in cherry-blossom time!" That is the season Hiroshige chose for his depiction of Shushoin.

14. Landscaped Gardens at the Nippori Temple

Nippori jiin-no rinsen (2/1857)

Celebrated Buddhist monasteries and Shinto shrines attracted Hiroshige: a considerable proportion of the prints in the series are devoted to such places. Yet very often he did not depict the buildings themselves, but the adjoining precincts. The holy place is not presented as an architectural masterpiece or a historical relic, but as a part of the city whose life was the main theme of *A Hundred Famous Views of Edo.*

Here we find ourselves on the grounds of the Shinto shrine Suwa-myojin, which was held to protect two neighbouring places, Yanaka and Nippori (see No. 14). The latter appears in the print: a fairly steep slope leads to a group of buildings half-hidden by masses of cherry-blossom.

The Suwa-myojin shrine was founded in 1205. It became the object of particular attention in the fifteenth century when Ota Dokan (1432-1486), the builder of the first castle at Edo, granted it land. Later visitors were to a large extent attracted by the views to be had from the Suwanodai promontory. It is one of these views that Hiroshige presents: looking out into the distance across broad rice paddies to where the twin-peaked Mount Tsukuba (see No. 36) and the Nikko range to its left rise.

Hiroshige far from always adhered to the true proportions and shape of mountains. Almost all the depictions of Tsukubayama (which appears eleven times in the series), for example, inaccurately show the western ("male") summit to be higher than the eastern ("female") one. For Hiroshige and his contemporaries it was not so important to be absolutely accurate in the depiction of a mountain, but rather to provide the correct visual key which prompted identification of the image with the real-life prototype and evoked a stream of associations and recollections, both literary and historical.

15. Suwa Bluff at Nippori

Nippori Suwanodai (5/1856)

It is believed that the name Sendagi – "1000 Bundles of Firewood" – came from the trade practised by the local peasants: they cut firewood in the surrounding woods and then brought it to Edo 1000 bundles at a time. This formerly rural area was only incorporated into the city in 1745.

The area was made famous by Dangozaka ("Dumpling Slope"), the most celebrated feature of its kind in Edo. The name reflects the fact that dumplings had traditionally been sold here. It was noted for the beauty of the surrounding countryside and the view far out across Edo Bay and the low-lying city.

Hiroshige's print depicts grounds where plum and cherry trees grew, as well as flowers that bloomed successively throughout all four seasons. There was also a lotus pond on the far bank of which the artist places us.

In the upper part of the print a steep flight of steps, flanked by stone lamps and artificial rocks, leads up to a tall pavilion. This is the *hanayashiki* or "pavilion of flowers", properly known as *Shisentei*, the "Pavilion of the Purple Spring". The pavilion, which stood to the south of Dangozaka, had three storeys and was unusually tall for a building of this type. The visitors looking out of the second and third storey windows are enjoying a view of Ueno Hill and the Shinobazu-no ike pond.

Space in this print is divided by stylized clouds like those frequently found in ancient Japanese painting. The band of cloud draws such a firm boundary between the lower and upper scenes that it might seem that the artist has depicted two different places in one picture. In reality that is not the case. There has to be another reason for this compositional structure so unusual for Hiroshige's series. Possibly correct is the suggestion sometimes put forward by scholars that here the artist presented one and the same place, but at different seasons of the year: spring below and autumn above. This might be taken as an affirmation of another name popularly given to Shisentei – "the Pavilion of the Flowers of the Four Seasons".

16. The Pavilion of Flowers on Dangozaka Slope,
the Sendagi Quarter

Sendagi Dangozaka Hanayashiki (5/1856)

Admiring the cherry blossoms was one of the most traditional and popular pastimes for the Japanese in the nineteenth century and remains so today. Four places were most frequented for *hanami*: Ueno (see No. 11), Gotenyama (see No. 28), the bank of the Sumidagawa and Asukayama, the hill depicted in this print.

The name of the hill came from a small Shinto shrine that was founded as early as 1321-1324. In the Kanyei era (1624-1644), when another shrine, Oji-gongen (see No. 19), was built to the north of the place depicted, it was moved to the very top of the hill.

In 1737, Yoshimune, the eighth shogun, granted the Asukayama area to the Buddhist Kinrinji monastery that was associated with a Shinto shrine in the shogun's native province (of which Oji-gongen in turn was a "daughter house"). To mark the event, Yoshimune ordered the planting of hundreds of cherry trees on Asukayama.

The resulting cherry orchard became the Eastern Capital's first public park: a government decree granted free access to the monastery grounds.

Soon teahouses and other places of amusement appeared at the foot of the hill. Despite being over three miles from the centre of the city, it became one of the most popular places to spend time in the bosom of nature, particularly in the cherry-blossom season.

Visitors sit on mats spread out on a promontary rising above flooded rice paddies with Mount Tsukuba dominant in the distance. By tradition cherry-viewing was accompanied by other amusements: the little parties drink sake, two rather tipsy men have tucked up the hems of their kimonos to perform a dance with fans.

On the very edge of the hill an elderly woman and a child are engaged in another traditional pastime: tossing small clay plates into the wind.

17. The View North from Asukayama Hill

Asukayama kita-no chobo (5/1856)

In this print we are in the same small area as in the previous one, all we have done is move to a different slope of Asukayama, to the precincts of the Oji Inari-jinja. The mountain in the distance is still Tsukubayama, but from a slightly different angle.

Oji Inari-jinja was an ancient shrine going back to before the Edo period and was well preserved. A new main building and gate were built in 1808 and have come down to the present without significant alterations.

Inari, originally a harvest deity, was later redefined as the bringer of prosperity and success in one's affairs, including commerce. The Inari cult, originally agricultural, began to spread into urban areas roughly in the first half of the eighteenth century.

An almost invariable attribute of Inari was the vixen, the messenger of the deity, frequently identified with it. In early times shrines to Inari were built in forests or on hills remote from human habitation. Inari-jinja too, the chief centre of the cult in Kanto (eastern Honshu island), was located in the suburban village of Oji. Such places abounded in foxes and there were certainly many on Asukayama. Perhaps this led to the belief that on the last day of the year all the foxes from the surrounding area gathered at the shrine and assumed the appearance of courtly beauties. In Far Eastern folklore foxes were considered magical beings capable of changing their appearance (see No. 118).

The deeds of foxes in human guise were a very common theme in folk tales and parables. They often appeared in the visual arts too: in prints, netsuke and lacquer work. One of them, directly connected with the Oji shrine, was a favourite with the storytellers (*rakugoka*) who could be found at the crossroads of the capital.

Once a young man heading for Oji Inari-jinja saw a vixen at the instant when she was changing into a woman. The man was taken by her beauty and invited her to join him in the nearest tavern.

During the meal the vixen got tipsy and returned to her natural appearance. She was brought back to her senses by a servant driving her out of the place with a broom. The vixen fled. The next day the young man felt guilty and decided to make amends. He bought some sweetmeats and began calling the vixen from her lair. A cub came out, listened to his apologies and took the peace offering to his mother. The vixen now assumed the role of a caring mother, instilling caution in her children. Looking at the sweetmeats, she raised an eyebrow and said suspiciously: "Take care, it might be horse dung!"

Once a year, during the temple festival on the 1st Day of the Horse in the Second Month, the shrine was associated with something else. The day was known as the kite fair (*tako-no ichi*). This festival too had an agricultural origin, as a ritual to protect the coming harvest. The event retained a similar character in the Edo period, but it was supposed to bring protection not so much from natural disasters as from a very real, very common enemy of urban life – fire.

All visitors to the shrine on this day were each given a protective kite with special talismanic symbols on the "wings". They were supposed to take it home and put it in the main room (*zashiki*), after which, it was believed, they need not fear fire.

The choice of the Second Month for such a ritual was quite appropriate. In Kanto, the weather at that time is dry and windy, greatly increasing the risk of fire.

Hiroshige's print shows the precincts of the shrine in early spring. The plum-trees beyond Inari-jinja have just begun to open. In all probability this is one of the days of the First Month of the year. The visitors, peasants and city dwellers, have come to pray for prosperity in the New Year. They climb the stone steps leading from the torii gate to the main building of the shrine, where they are met by a priest dressed in ceremonial robes.

18. The Inari Shrine at Oji

Oji Inari-no yashiro (9/1857)

This dam was built in 1657 for irrigation purposes to the north of Asukayama (see No. 17). Otonashigawa is the name of part of a river, which as a whole is customarily called the Shakujii. It begins in the Sanpoji-no ike pond in Musashi province and flows into the Arakawa river. It is known as Otonashigawa, the "Noiseless River", in the vicinity of the Oji-gongen shrine (see No. 49).

The name is rather circuitously due to that shrine. Shogun Yoshimune (see No. 17) declared Oji-gongen to be a "daughter house" of Kumano-gongen in his native province and since that shrine stood on the Otonashi River, the stretch of the Shakujii below Asukayama acquired the same name. The Kinrinji monastery, whose buildings can be seen behind the dam, was the Buddhist "patron" of two neighbouring Shinto shrines: Oji-gongen and Oji Inari-jinja (see No. 18).

During the Edo period, the monastery enjoyed the particular attention of the Tokugawa family, but in the Meiji period it was abandoned and today only two of its buildings, originally of minor importance, still exist. One of them, the temple of the Buddha Amida, is depicted in the middle distance here.

The water spilling over the dam was commonly referred to as Otaki, "the Great Waterfall". In actual fact, it was considerably more modest in size than is shown here. Possibly not only compositional considerations, but also the popular name prompted Hiroshige to exaggeration.

19. The Dam on the Otonashi River at Oji, Popularly Known as "The Great Waterfall"

Oji Otonashigawa entai sezoku Otaki to tonau (2/1857)

This ferry across the Sumidagawa was in the northern outskirts of Edo. It served pilgrims seeking to visit the Zenkoji monastery. Hiroshige has depicted three such pilgrims on the left bank of the river. They are making for the jetty, which is not visible in the print. On the other hand, we can see the ferry itself with four passengers halfway to the far bank, close to which stand the red buildings of Zenkoji, half-hidden by the cartouche containing the title.

Kawaguchi was noted for the production of metal tableware: tea kettles, jugs and wine flasks. But its main claim to fame was the monastery belonging to the Tendai school. It was a "daughter house" and namesake of a famous religious centre in Shinano province, one of the most ancient shrines in Japan. There is a legend attached to the foundation of Zenkoji close to the future Edo – Tokyo. Once a monk named Teison was visited in his sleep by the Amida Buddha venerated in Zenkoji (Shinano province) who instructed the monk to make an exact image of him. Teison collected funds to pay for the casting of a statue and moulded a sculptural group of three figures:

the Amida Buddha and two accompanying bodhisattvas, Kannon and Seishi. This work was completed in 1195 and the composition was placed in a temple, which became known as Zenkoji.

For two months every seventeen years the monks here allowed the visiting laity to view the sculpture. The ceremony was known as "the raising of the curtain" (*kaicho*), although in reality it consisted of opening the doors on the reliquary (*zushi*) in which the statue was kept. The *kaicho* at Zenkoji attracted large crowds and was accompanied by theatrical performances and shows by wandering magicians and acrobats. The sides of the road leading to the monastery became open-air gambling dens. Games of chance were forbidden, but at Kawaguchi once in seventeen years, the authorities turned a blind eye to such goings-on.

This print was issued in the Second Month of 1857, exactly a year before the next kaicho was due. It was, therefore, a sort of advertisement or advance notice of a festival beloved of all the inhabitants of the capital.

20. The Zenkoji Monastery by the Kawaguchi Ferry

Kawaguchi-no watashi Zenkoji (2/1857)

Mount Atago stands to the east of Yamanote, an aristocratic section of the city containing the mansions of *daimyo* and high-ranking samurai. It got its name from the Atago-jinja or Atago-gongen shrine constructed on its summit, which in turn was named after the celebrated Atago-jinja in Kyoto, where Raijin, the god of thunder, was venerated as a protector against fire. Daughter houses of the Kyoto shrine could be found across the country, including this one at Shiba. It was founded at the same time as its Buddhist "opposite number", the Enpukuji monastery situated at the foot of Mount Atago.

In 1603 Tokugawa Ieyasu built a shrine on its summit and in it he placed a statue of a deity that he esteemed highly exceptional – Shogun Jizo, a bodhisattva of Xitigarbhi the Bringer-of-Victory. It was said that Ieyasu's impassioned prayer to that deity helped him to win the Battle of Sekigahara (1600). Two flights of steps lead up to the shrine. The steeper one, with eighty-six steps, is known as the "male slope"; the gentler climb of 108 steps to one side is the "female slope".

There is a story associated with the male slope. One day in 1634 Shogun Iemitsu was returning from Zojoji, where he had paid his respects at the grave of his father Kidetada on the second anniversary of his death, when he noticed a large plum tree in blossom on the top of the hill. He challenged his guards to ride to it up the steeper steps, cut off a branch and come down by the same route. Many tried, but only one young warrior, named Magaki Heikuro, succeeded. This story became the subject of popular tales (*kodan*) and Magaki Heikuro's name gradually turned into a common noun referring to a skilful horseman. Interestingly, attempts to repeat his feat have been made in much more recent times. Three riders have emulated him: in 1882, 1925 and 1982.

In early times there was a monthly pilgrimage to Mount Atago in Shiba. More famous, however, was the "thousand-day pilgrimage" (*sennichi-mode*), which took place on the 24th day of the Sixth Month. Originally this practice matched its name: an almost three-year journey around the Buddhist monasteries and Shinto shrines located in various corners of the country. In the Edo period, however, the custom was changed: a visit to one particular temple or another was declared "equivalent" to three years of wandering. In the Eastern Capital, the *sennichi-mode* could be accomplished in two places: at Sensoji on the 10th day of the Seventh Month, and at Atago-jinja, half a month earlier.

The most famous and popular festival at Atago-jinja was called Bishamon-matsuri and dedicated to Bishamon-ten, the guardian of the North in the Buddhist pantheon and one of the seven gods of happiness in popular beliefs.

This ceremony takes place on the 3rd day of the First Month and takes the form of a ritual of prayer for an abundant harvest, prosperity and happiness in the New Year. A group of the laity took part in the procession, led by the "messenger of Bishamon", who was usually "played" by the owner of the Agatoya tea-house located on the top of the hill. In the early afternoon this messenger led a procession out of the main building of the shrine (*honsha*) and descended the "male slope" to Enpukuji. In the monastery he ceremonially consumed a dish of rice and red beans (*kowameshi*), after which he returned to the shrine by the gentler, "female slope".

It was the culminating moment of this ritual that Hiroshige depicted. The whole foreground of the print is occupied by a corner of the shrine and the figure of the "messenger", ascending the last of the 108 steps. He holds an immense paddle for rice (*shaku*) with which he knocks on a chopping-board about ten feet long during the ceremony and carries a huge pestle in his belt. Fastened to his robe are strips of edible seaweed (*konbu*), which the participants in the ceremony will eat afterwards. His costume is topped off by a helmet in the form of an inverted bowl with a mandarin (*daidai*), a traditional New Year decoration, attached to it. The fronds of fern hanging down from the brim also have a seasonal propitiatory significance. Besides all this, behind his back is a pole crowned with a sacred ornament of paper strips (*gohei*). The entire figure is assembled from symbols of prosperity, wealth and success.

It is interesting that in this instance Hiroshige was particularly concerned to identify the subject of the print: above his own signature he inserted an additional text: "shogatsu mikka Bishamon zukai" – "the messenger of Bishamon on the 3rd day of the First Month". In the top left-hand corner, on a piece of board which usually bore the names of those who had made donations to the shrine, he indicated the time of the ceremony "on the fortuitous day [...] month, 1857".

The unusual location of the title in one cartouche with the signature means that it can be read as "Painted by Hiroshige, the messenger of Bishamon on the 3rd day of the First Month". The upper date adds the year. This has prompted some scholars to consider the "messenger" a self-portrait.

Behind the main figure we have a view of Shibaura Bay (see No. 108) and the city sprawl from which the high roof of the main temple in the Tsukiji Honganji monastery (see No. 78) stands out.

Atago-jinja was also noted for its "seasonal" attractions: in spring it was customary to admire the cherry blossoms here; in autumn, to observe the moon.

21. Mount Atago, the Shiba District

Shiba Atagoyama (8/1857)

Up until the mid-nineteenth century Hiroo, or more exactly Hiroo-ga hara ("the Hiroo Plain") was a rural locality in the Shibuya district to the north-west of Edo.

Unworked areas of land, overgrown with the plant known as mare's tail (*tsukushi* – hence the older name Tsukushi-no hara), alternated with the mansions of high-ranking samurai. Only towards the very end of the Edo period did people begin to build teahouses and restaurants at Hiroo. It became a destination for day-trippers out to see "untouched nature".

Hiroo was adjacent to a small river called the Furukawa (as is almost always the case with rivers in Edo, the name applied only to the upper part of its course). The print shows the stretch of river where it flows under the Shinohashi or Fourth Bridge, which was sometimes called the Sagamidono-hashi or Bridge of the Lord of Sagami, since the house of the ruler of that province stood here at one time. One feature of Hiroo that particularly fascinated townspeople was the watermills located along the Furukawa.

In the 1850s the main attraction of Hiroo was the restaurant originally called Owariya, which stood where Hiroshige depicted it, on the left bank of the Furukawa. The speciality of the house was an eel dish highly prized in the Eastern Capital and the establishment became popularly known as Kitsune unagi ("The Vixen's Eel"). This second name became so firmly attached to the place that it appears on an official map of Edo dating from 1854.

22. The Furukawa River at Hiroo

Hiroo Furukawa (7/1856)

In Hiroshige's time, Meguro was part of the quiet outskirts of forests and fields. From time to time the shoguns practised falconry here, while in spring the peasants gathered young bamboo shoots which they sold by the gate of the Ryusenji monastery.

The common people's name for this Tendai-school monastery – Meguro Fudo ("Black-Eyed Fudo") – attached itself to the whole locality.

The history of the monastery goes back to the time of Ieyasu and his great advisor Tenkai, the monk who founded Kanyeiji (see No. 11). Tenkai believed that the new capital should be protected by divine forces as well as men and he gave instructions for the building of five outlying monasteries, each of which was dedicated to Fudo-Myoo, an awesome guardian deity. The statues of Fudo installed in them differed in the colour of the eyes. Meguro Fudo was the largest of the monasteries and considered the most important, although there are no notable sights here.

Even the waterfall, which dropped in stages into the Chiyogaike pond (it existed until the 1930s) was never particularly famous, nor was the pond itself, named after a certain O-Chiyo, the wife of a samurai who drowned herself in it after her husband died in battle.

It is hard to say how accurately Hiroshige reproduced the actual appearance of this spot. It is obvious, however, that he strove to create an image of early spring on the outskirts of the Eastern Capital. For that reason, he paid particular attention to such things as conveying the reflection of the trees in the pond, a device to which he rarely resorted. This technically complex device came into *ukiyo-e* from European painting and had been fully assimilated.

It has even less of a "borrowed" feel to it than the linear perspective which in Hiroshige's landscapes fitted harmoniously into the spatial structure specific to the *ukiyo-e* print.

23. The Chiyogaike Pond at Meguro

Meguro Chiyogaike (7/1856)

At Meguro there were two structures connected with one of the most popular cults in Japanese folk religion, that of Mount Fuji. One of them, Shin-Fuji ("New Fuji"), is shown here.

The cult of Fuji has its roots in mythological time. Pilgrimages up the mountain began in the ninth century and by the Edo period had become generally practised. People ascended to venerate the deity of the Fuji-gongen shrine, located on the very peak, between the 1st and 21st days of the Sixth Month each year.

In the early seventeenth century, the cult of Fuji became exceptionally popular in urban and rural circles. The devotee Kakugyo Tobutsu (1541-1646) developed it into a distinct religious movement in its own right with the mountain being worshipped as a deity called Sengen-dainichi. The movement took on organized form and adepts came together in special groups (*fujiko*). Dressed in white robes, they climbed the mountain ringing bells and chanting sacred verses.

Women did not take part in the ascent for ritual reasons, while it was too much of a strain for children, the elderly and the sick. For that reason, in the second part of the eighteenth century people began erecting miniature copies of Fujiyama, which were used for the same purposes as the original. The first artificial Fuji (*fuji-zuka*) appeared in 1779 or 1780. *Edo meisho zue* describes its creator as "the great devotee Tojiro".

Sometimes the name Chujiro is given, but in all probability it is the same individual.

The season of pilgrimages to such artificial Fujis varied from place to place around Edo. It was usually in the Fifth or Sixth Month, most often from the 15th to the 18th day of the latter.

The New Fuji at Meguro that Hiroshige depicted in the present print was raised in 1829. It took the form of an earth mound overgrown with grass. This set it apart from other fuji-zuka, which were usually assembled from lumps of lava collected on the real Fuji and therefore had a more angular shape. A characteristic feature of the artificial Fujis was a zigzag path leading to the top and a model of a vertical rock halfway up. Both existed on the real-life prototype. The rock was called Eboshi, the "Hat Rock", since it was shaped like the tall headwear worn at court.

The New Fuji afforded a superb view of the real Fujiyama and the surrounding countryside. In Hiroshige's print it is being enjoyed by pilgrims who have reached the summit. Below stands the noted temple of Meguro Fudo. The composition is simple and effective with the space being organized by the peaks of the two Fujis. The confident diagonal is also stressed by colour: each of the peaks is accentuated by a bright cartouche, the one containing the artist's signature, the other the title of the series and print.

24. New Fuji at Meguro

Meguro Shin-Fuji (4/1857)

Two *fuji-zuka* were put up at Meguro in the early part of the nineteenth century. The New Fuji, featured in the preceding print, was new in relation to the other artificial mountain constructed 17 years earlier, in 1812, less than a mile to the north. After the appearance of a second *fuji-zuka*, the older mound became known as Moto-Fuji, "the Original Fuji".

The way in which Moto-Fuji was landscaped betrays a desire to make it look picturesque. It is the only *fuji-zuka* in Edo where the path to the summit is marked by pines planted at regular intervals. Moto-Fuji was intended not so much as a setting for the practice of religious ritual as a pleasant place to spend time admiring the views across the water-meadows of the Megurogawa river. At the foot of the mound tea-pavilions were specially set up among the cherry trees for this purpose and they are partially shown in the print. In the contents page of the series this print is placed in the "Spring" section, but doubts about the correctness of this immediately arise on seeing the yellow foliage of the trees (even allowing for the possible decomposition of pigments) and the dense, dark shade of green on the slope. The costumes of the pilgrims as well are noticeably too thick for spring, a warm, even hot season.

All the indications are that what we have here is an autumnnal view of Moto-Fuji which found its way into the "Spring" section if not through carelessness, then through the whim of the compiler who thought it interesting to place the depictions of the two *fuji-zuka* at Meguro next to each other.

25. The Original Fuji at Meguro

Meguro Moto-Fuji (4/1857)

This print is a rare example of how in the course of the series Hiroshige "left the capital", depicting its more distant outskirts. The setting is the shore of the bay. Edo, with the peak of the volcano Nikko-zan rising above it, can be divined in the shapes of the far shore in the lower part of the print. Further to the right we see the silhouette of the Chiba peninsula.

Edo meisho zue states: "If one looks from here, then the sea opens to one's gaze, the view is exceptionally beautiful." The attractiveness of the prospects on all sides of the hill gave it its name – Hakkeizaka, meaning "the Slope of Eight [*i.e.* many] Views".

When Hiroshige created his series, the sea came in close to the foot of the hill and the Tokaido highway lay along the shore. This was the section in which it finally escaped from the city and its outskirts. The Shinagawa, the point where those seeing travellers off took their leave, was already passed. That was a lively spot with a large number of leisure establishments and shops ranged along the shore (see No. 28). Shinagawa is present in this print too: it is the headland sticking out quite a way into the bay tightly packed with houses that we see on the left-hand side.

In Hiroshige's time, Hakkeizaka was adorned by a gigantic pine of eccentric shape. The tree was quite a noted landmark. Travellers on the Tokaido made a stop here to drink tea or have a bite in one of the eating-houses situated alongside the pine, despite the fact that it meant a detour and an uphill climb. The bizarre pine was worth the effort, like the view from Hakkeizaka.

It was more than just part of the landscape. The very name "Hanging-Armour Pine" evoked associations with Japan's martial past. There was a legend that, during his campaign against the insurgent Abe-no Sadato (1019-1062), Hatimantaro Yoshiie (1041-1108), the outstanding military commander of the late Heian period, stopped to rest here and hung his armour on one of the pines.

By Hiroshige's day, that pine would have been about eight hundred years old and we do not know whether there was in fact such an old tree on the hill. It is, however, clear that the artist altered the shape and size of the tree. *Edo meisho zue* mentions its having exceptionally long, widely spreading branches. Its dimensions were no less impressive: a height of 6-7 *jo* (some sixty feet) and a trunk so thick that, had there been an opening, it could have contained an ox. Once again Hiroshige breaks with documentary accuracy, making the tree more slender and giving it an elegant curve in the trunk in order, as is sometimes observed, to make it visually resemble the "hook" on which Yoshiie once hung his armour.

26. The "Hanging-Armour Pine" and Hakkeizaka

Hakkeizaka Yoroikakematsu (5/1856)

The Kamata district was particularly noted for its abundant plum trees, which created an attractive spectacle when they blossomed in early spring. Horticulturally Kamata reached the peak of its fame in the Bunsei era (1818-1830) when a special garden was laid out in the grounds of Namekata Danjo's house, which became known as Umeyashiki, the "Plum Mansion".

Despite being private property, the garden was open to the public: teahouses, taverns and leisure establishments appeared here. Some of them, such as the tea-house on the bank of a pond in the shape of a gourd (which still exists), feature in Hiroshige's print.

Apart from its aesthetic quality, the garden also had a practical function. The fruit was used to make pickles and marinades, primarily marinaded plums (*umeboshi*) which was a very popular hot flavouring for rice sold at the city markets. The main product derived from plums was, however, the medicine called wachusan, which travellers took in hot weather to ward off sunstroke and dizziness.

Placed sharply in the foreground is part of a *yamakago* (literally "mountain palanquin"), a mode of transport extensively used in the Edo period. A section of a palanquin in the foreground juxtaposed with the more distant image was typical of the series. Here though, the appearance of a palanquin among the strollers in the garden is somewhat unusual. It is explicable, however, since Umeyashiki was close to the Tokaido and travellers on the highway were able to make a brief stop to admire the plums in blossom.

27. The Plum Orchard in Kamata

Kamata-no umezono (2/1857)

The Shinagawa district held a special attraction for Hiroshige. In *A Hundred Famous Views of Edo*, he depicts the sights of the area and various aspects of its life with surprising persistence. Life here was to a large extent determined by the fact that Shinagawa was the starting point for those heading for Kyoto, Nara and Osaka on the Tokaido highway.

Distances were customarily measured from the Nihonbashi (see No. 1), but in reality a traveller took his leave of the Eastern Capital in the south-western suburb. Here he parted with friends, who by tradition gave him a proper send-off (which took some time), before starting on his way.

Shinagawa was marked by two eminences – Yatsuyama and Gotenyama. The latter translates as "Palace Hill" and for several centuries there really was a palace on the hill. After Tokugawa Ieyasu made Edo the new capital, the palace was reconstructed and, from the Kanyei era (1624-1644) onwards, it was used as a hunting lodge by the Tokugawa shoguns.

The new palace did not last long: it burnt down in the Genroku era (1688-1704). Slightly earlier, Gotenyama was planted with cherry trees and it became a favourite place to admire the blossom.

Edo meisho zue states: "In the Third Month, when the cherry trees are in full bloom, they are like clouds or can be confused with snow. The scent of the flowers is carried a long way by the sea breeze and impregnates even the sleeves of the coastal inhabitants who collect seafood here when the tide is out."

In Hiroshige's time Gotenyama, the sea and the cherry trees were perceived as a single whole as is shown by a then-celebrated poem:
Gotenyama hill!
The cherries fly from it
Straight into the sea.

Or another, that might be taken as a parody of the panegyric to the blooming cherry trees in *Edo meisho zue*.
And as far as Gotenyama
The wind carries
The "scent" of fresh fish.

A few years before Hiroshige created his series, the appearance of Gotenyama changed radically. The arrival of Commodore Perry's "black ships" in 1853 forced the government to think of coastal defences. A series of eleven forts equipped with artillery was planned. Work began immediately after Perry's departure and within a year five forts were already complete, another two half-finished. But at that point the work was suspended.

The earth for the forts was taken from Gotenyama and the traces can be clearly seen in Hiroshige's print. But the cherries are still in blossom. They were destined to disappear later, in 1870-1871 when the first railway in Japan was laid across Gotenyama.

28. The Gotenyama in Shinagawa

Shinagawa Gotenyama (4/1856)

In the Edo period the name Sunamura referred to an area adjoining Edo Bay, delineated on the other three sides by rivers and canals – the Arakawa drainage canal and the Nakagawa river on the east, the Konakigawa canal on the north and the Jikkengawa canal on the west. The area lay beneath the sea until in 1659 Sunamura Shinjiro carried out work to drain part of the bay. The reclaimed land was named after him.

There were rice paddies here, protected by dykes on which pines and cherry trees were grown. On the other side of the dyke, the Nakagawa river flows through the marshes, while in the distance we see the mouth of the Edogawa, flowing into Edo Bay and the hills of the Chiba peninsula.

Hiroshige avoided directly presenting the place which, according to the title was the main subject of the print.

We can see only the stone gate that marked the approach to the Moto-Hachiman Shrine from the south and an ancillary building "overwritten" by the red cartouche containing the artist's signature.

Hiroshige uses a device which we might term the "being there" effect: the viewer is presented with the view to be had from the temple precincts.

By the early nineteenth century Moto-Hachiman had become a place for the inhabitants of Edo to stroll. Shops and teahouses appeared here, while "monuments" were set up to amuse the public.

Some of the latter have survived, such as a stone plaque inscribed with a work by Matsuo Basho (1644-1699), a popular poet of the Edo period.

29. Moto-Hachiman Shrine, Sunamura

Sunamura Moto-Hachiman (4/1856)

In the Edo period Kameido still lay outside the city. The easiest way to reach it was by water, along the Jikkengawa canal past Yanagishima with its noted temple to the bodhisattva Myoken and Hashimotoya teahouse (see No. 32). Travelling a few hundred yards further, you reached the Kameido-tenjin shrine and Kameido Umeyashiki, the celebrated plum orchard.

The beauty of the trees in blossom and their scent was noted by Shogun Yoshimune, who travelled in these parts in 1720.

One unusual plum tree was particularly famous – the Garyubai ("Reclining Dragon"). This tree is the subject of Hiroshige's print: although at first sight there seems to be a whole orchard here, it is all the one Garyubai.

The tree died after a flood in 1880. The memorial plaque that stands where it grew reads: "On this site during the Edo period Kiemon, the owner of the plot, laid out a plum orchard and called it Umeyashiki or Seikoan ["The Scented Refuge of Purity"]. The orchard became famous as a place for amusements and contemplation of the plum blossom.

It contained a celebrated plum tree whose branches looked like a reclining dragon: they hung down and went underground, then re-emerged a considerable distance away, forming a new trunk. There is a story that the name Reclining Dragon was given to this tree by Mito Mitsukuni." Tokugawa Mitsukuni (1627-1700) belonged to a side branch of the ruling house. He was head of the Mito clan and an outstanding historian. Possibly in giving the unusual tree such a name he was comparing it with himself. One of his names was Shiryu ("Little Dragon") and his pseudonym was go-Bairi ("Plum Tree").

In Hiroshige's day the extensive area over which the plum tree grew was fenced off. The visitors who came to admire it in blossom had to do so from a distance.

This print, like number 58, was destined to play a role in the history of Western painting. Vincent van Gogh copied it, studying the visual devices, compositional structure and emotional charge of *ukiyo-e* prints, which at that time were perceived as the most characteristically Japanese art form.

30. The Plum Orchard in Kameido

Kameido Umeyashiki (11/1857)

Despite the title, the real subject of this print is the Jikkengawa canal, with cherry trees evenly spaced along its bank. Jikkengawa means "the Ten-Ken River" (1 *ken* = 6 feet). In reality it was a canal, dug out in the Manji era (1856-1860) to link the Sumidagawa and Nakagawa, the two most important rivers in the Eastern Capital. This short, fairly narrow watercourse thus became an element of particular importance in Edo's waterborne transport system.

The composition is arranged so that the viewer's eye is drawn along the bank, past rice paddies, to the Shinto shrine in the depths of the picture. Azuma-no mori, whose entrance is marked by a stone gateway, was devoted to the worship of the deity Ototachibanahime-no mikoto. She was the wife of Prince Yamato Takeru-no mikoto, a mythological warrior who subdued the eastern parts of Honshu. The word Azuma has a legendary explanation. When Yamato Takeru was crossing what would become Edo Bay in boats a storm blew up. In order to appease the elements, his spouse sacrificed herself by leaping into the water. When he reached the shore safely, the Prince looked back to where she had died and exclaimed "Aa tsuma" – "Oh, my wife!". This was taken up as Azuma and became a poetic name for all the eastern provinces, and for the East in general. The word features in the names of many structures and settlements close to the shrine, such as the Azumabashi bridge (see No. 39).

The legend goes on to account for the main curiosity of the place, Renri-no kusu, a camphor tree with one root but two trunks that had grown together. (The title, it must be noted, names another kind of tree, the *azusa* or catalpa, but that is obviously a "slip of the pen": the characters for *azusa* and *kusu* (camphor) differ only in a few elements which were probably omitted due to haste.)

A few days after the Princess's death, the waves deposited her comb on shore. It was buried beneath a small mound. The inconsolable Yamato Takeru stuck a pair of chopsticks made of camphor wood into the mound and thought to himself that if they grew, he would manage to bring order to the country. And so it happened.

According to another story, the tree with one root and two stems, the "male" and the "female", was a symbol of conjugal love which even death could not destroy. This interpretation is "taken up" by other place names in the vicinity, such as Tsumagoizaki – the "Slope of Love towards the Wife".

The Renri-no kusu was regarded as a miracle-working tree, the dwelling-place of a deity, which could heal a variety of ailments. *Edo meisho hana goyomi* ("A Flowery Calendar of the Sights of Edo") states: "The sick offer prayers to the deity Azuma-gongen. If you ask the local anchorite for leaves of the camphor tree, make an infusion of them and drink it, then you will certainly recover. [The deity] is especially well disposed towards prayers for deliverance from convulsions. Accordingly many people set up flags before this deity in gratitude for being cured."

The tree is depicted in the centre of the print, surrounded by pilgrims gazing at the bizarre double trunk. It was nowhere near as large as it is shown here. We know that the trunk split at a height of four *shaku* (about four feet), while in the print it divides about fifteen feet up. The general look of the landscape is authentic. Hiroshige exaggerates details, a device consciously employed in the series with the aim of stressing the most meaningful element of the picture. The reddening sky is an indication that evening is approaching: the blossoming cherries along the canal point again to spring.

31. The Conjoined Camphor Trees by the Azuma-no Mori Shrine

Azuma-no mori Renri-no azusa (7/1856)

Hiroshige shows us a built-up area at the junction of two canals. The Kita-Jikkengawa (Northern Sixty-Foot River) running from top to bottom is crossed at right-angles by the Yoko-Jikkengawa (Parallel Sixty-Foot River). These waterways played a substantial role in the transport system of the Northern Capital, linking a network of rivers and canals to the Sumidagawa, the city's main artery.

The village of Yanagishima, which was here in the early seventeenth century, was absorbed into the city in 1713. The occasion was the construction of a new bridge linking it with the centre.

The bridge was called Yanigabashi, the "Willow Bridge", although a bridge of that name already existed (see No. 5).

Soon the area around the bridge became one of the liveliest amusement centres for the capital's populace. It was from here that boats departed for the "pleasure quarters" of Fukagawa and Shin-Yoshiwara (see No. 38), as well as to Mukojima (see No. 39).

Here too establishments sprang up whose beautiful hostesses took part not only in festive meals, but, most notably, in waterborne amusements in boats (*funeasobi*).

The most well known establishment in Yanagishima was called simply as Hashimotoya ("By the Bridge"). This was a first-class place intended mainly for large banquets and Hiroshige makes it the "central character" of the work. The brightly lit building is in the middle of the composition, right at the end of the bridge.

To the left is Yanagishima's most notable sight, the Myokendo temple in the Nichiren monastery of Hoshoji (Myokenzan). This temple was dedicated to the bodhisattva Myoken, an embodiment of the constellation of the Great Bear, worshipped as the defender of the country, a deity giving protection from fire and granting people long life and happiness.

32. Yanagishima

Yanagishima (4/1857)

This print takes us into the distant north-western approaches to Edo. There is nothing here to remind us of the lively bustle that marks the artist's "urban" compositions. Perhaps there is no other print in the series that accords so precisely with its "programme" – to show the life of the city in all its manifestations. In Edo everything is interesting from start to finish. And a city starts with its outskirts.

The canal depicted was created in the early seventeenth century to supply the Fukagawa district with drinking water. A hundred years later it was used only for irrigation and as a means of conveying freight, mainly agricultural produce. In time, pleasure boats also appeared – little barges carrying two or three passengers and drawn by a man walking on the bank.

The destination might have been Kameari-mura shown in the print. The village was famous as a hunting centre for the shoguns with a special palace from which the ruler could observe the cranes, which nested in large numbers here. Commoners also came to watch the "crane dance". The Kameari-mura jetty is shown in the upper left-hand corner and we can just make out tiny figures alighting from the barges.

The boat trip was something of an attraction in itself. The use of "human traction" excited the Edoans' well-developed curiosity. In reality, it was a case of making a virtue of a necessity – the canal was shallow and only ten feet wide.

It extended another six miles to the north beyond Kameari-mura. In the print the narrow strip of water seems to reach the foot of the mountain dominating the scene. This is most often taken to be Tsukubayama, but Hiroshige might have intended one of the peaks of the Nikko range.

33. Tow-Boats on the Yotsugidori Canal

Yotsugidori yosui hikifune (2/1857)

For Hiroshige's contemporaries, Matsuyama was firmly connected with a visit to Yoshiwara, the most famous and expensive "green quarter" in Japan, which was noted for its beautiful courtesans.

In the Edo period it was customary to approach Yoshiwara by water. You could take a hired boat and turn from the Sumidagawa into the Sanyabori canal, which took you almost to your destination. You could also disembark earlier, by the Imadobashi bridge, which stood at the meeting-point of river and canal, to make your way to Yoshiwara on foot or in a palanquin along the Nihon-zutsumi ("Japan Dyke") that ran along the Sanyabori.

In 1619 some quarters of Asakusa were seriously affected by flooding of the Arakawa and in 1620 the dyke was raised on government orders to prevent a recurrence. *Daimyo* from all over Japan were involved in its construction, and this is one of the many explanations of the name. Until the late seventeenth century, the dyke was a deserted and fairly dangerous spot. Robbers were active there, as were *tsuji-giri* – "crossroads slashers", the name given to samurai or *ronin* itching to try their sword on a live opponent.

Eventually the government took measures and a guard-post was set up. In the Kyoho era (1716-1736) the place became more frequented, as the route to Yoshiwara, properly Shin-Yoshiwara ("New Yoshiwara"), lay alongside the Nihon-zutsumi.

Either side of the Imadobashi, which is prominent in the middle ground of the print, there was a noted restaurant: the lights of the Yumeiro can be seen to the left, those of the Takeya to the right.

Directly behind the Yumeiro Matsuchiyama looms up in the nocturnal gloom. In Hiroshige's work it is a fairly large and somewhat malevolent-looking hill. In reality it was a fairly low eminence, but it had a legend attached to its appearance.

It was said that during Empress Suiko's reign (592-628) the land swelled up and the Golden Dragon, the guardian of the hill, descended from the skies. Soon a monastery was founded here that came to be called Kinryuzan – the "Hill of the Golden Dragon". Kinryuzan is in reality one of the titles of the Sensoji monastery in Asakusa.

The temple on Matsuchiyama (which still exists) is called Honroin or, popularly, Matsuyama Shoten, and is a daughter house of the neighbouring Sensoji.

In Hiroshige's print we look at Matsuchiyama from the other bank of the Sumidagawa, which is called simply Mukojima, the "Island Opposite" – opposite Asakusa (see Nos. 53, 79, 99). Close to the spot depicted was the Mimeguri-jinja (see No. 39), a Shinto shrine noted for its cherry trees. One such tree frames the print on the right.

The geisha depicted in the foreground is probably returning from one of the entertainment establishments in the vicinity. She is following a servant who carries a lantern, part of which can be seen against the left-hand edge of the print. It is generally believed that the geisha is Hiroshige's beloved Koman.

The depiction of Matsuchiyama is the most expressive nocturnal landscape in the series. A black sky hangs over the entire watery scene. It glows with a host of stars, lit by a pulsating glow as if shining from within.

The sight of Matsuchiyama by night was celebrated among Hiroshige's contemporaries. There was a poem in circulation in Edo:
By Matsuchi hill the lights are bright
Perhaps they are stars, I thought
In the May rain.

34. Night View of Matsuchiyama and the Sanyabori Canal

Matsuchiyama Sanyabori yakei (8/1857)

Here Hiroshige takes us to Mukojima (see No. 39), which in his day was connected with the east bank of the Sumidagawa by the Hashiba-no watashi ferry (see No. 37).

The group in the foreground are making for the ferry. To their right a *torii* gate and two bronze lanterns mark the entrance to Suijin-no mori, which literally means "the Grove of the Water God". The word "grove" often occurs in the names of Shinto temples, a reminder of the times when the deified forces of nature were worshipped in a natural setting.

Suijin-no mori is dedicated to the Sumidagawa. Here they venerated the dragon who ruled the watery element, the defender and master of the river. The choice of site was no coincidence – at one time the mouth of the Sumidagawa was situated here. The viewer stands on the high bank, directly beneath a blossoming branch of a double-blossomed cherry tree (*yaezakura*). It flowers later than the ordinary Japanese cherry, and so we are into mid-spring here.

The place shown on the opposite bank is Massaki (see No. 36), which was noted for its shrines, first and foremost Massaki Inari-jinja, dedicated to the god of the harvest, and its teahouses.

The dominant element in the composition is Tsukubayama, depicted in the distance, almost in the centre of the page.

35. Massaki and the Suijin-no mori Shrine on the Sumidagawa

Sumidagawa Suijin-no mori Massaki (8/1856)

The "green quarters" of Yoshiwara were one of the most important sights of the Eastern Capital. Those going to Yoshiwara took their time; the journey itself was an amusement and a pleasure. A stop at Massaki was almost a "must".

The Shinto shrine here was not especially esteemed in the capital and the teahouses situated in front of the entrance were much more famous. Their speciality was *dengaku*, cubes of tofu impaled on sticks, coated with sweet bean paste and toasted over a charcoal brazier. The Kinoeneya was particularly noted for its food and Hiroshige places us in its upper storey.

Through the round window, the *shoji* shutters of which have not been completely opened, we have a view of the Sumidagawa and the opposite bank.

There, on a headland formed by the Sumidagawa and the little Uchigawa, we see an extensive grove with a *torii*-gate in front.

This grove contained the Suijin-no mori shrine (see No. 35). Over to the left are the houses of Sekiya-no sato, a fairly large settlement on the Sumidagawa, dominated by Tsukubayama behind.

The twin peaks of this mountain were known as "male" (western) and "female" (eastern). In myths, ancient tales and folk beliefs, it functioned as a symbol of unbreakable fidelity and all-conquering love. The mountain became a fixed poetic image. In the seventh-century Manyoshu ("A Collection of a Myriad Leaves"), the oldest Japanese anthology of poetry, the verse-makers often refer to Tsukuba. Here is just one example:

There, where Tsukuba's peak rose up,
On one side and the other,
Guards stand at posts everywhere.
Although mother guarded you and me,
We are still together in our hearts.

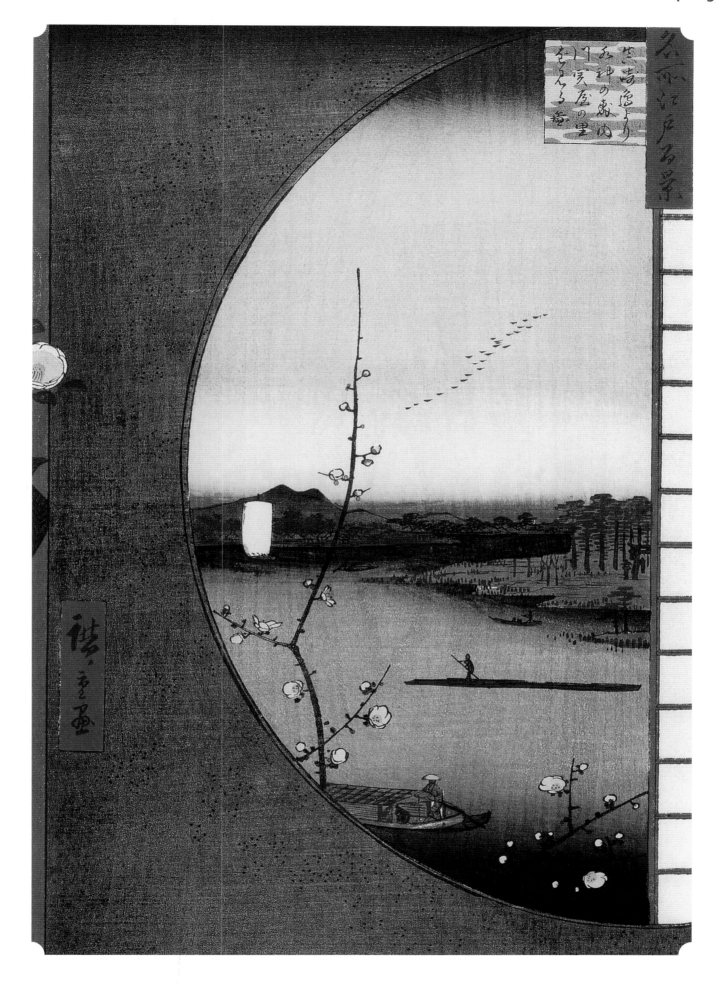

36. View from the Massaki Shrine of the Uchigawa Sekiya-no sato Village and the Suijin-no mori Shrine

Massaki-hen yori Suijin-no mori Utagawa Sekiya-no sato (8/1857)

Here Hiroshige places us in Asakusa on the west bank of the Sumidagawa. The artist might have crossed from Mikojima (see No. 39), the buildings of which with their distinctive yellow roofs are visible, together with the celebrated blossoming cherries, among the greenery on the other bank, using the ferry.

The print accurately shows two boats making the crossing, one in each direction. The name of the ferry is simply explained: *hashiba* means "by the bridge", and at one time there was indeed a bridge across the Sumidagawa here.

We find ourselves alongside the kilns that were used to bake tiles and simple pieces of pottery. These products were called *imado-yaki*, from the Imado area, which extended quite a way along the Sumidagawa. The tile-kilns were something of a landmark as they were fuelled with pine needles and constantly belched out smoke.

A family from the Chiba area came here as far back as the Tensho era (1573-1592) and constructed tile-kilns. Somewhat later, in the middle of the Edo period, the potters began producing small clay dolls as a sort of sideline and these rapidly became popular with the people of Edo.

Imado dolls fitted easily into the palm. They were usually painted in two colours: blue and red. Most frequently the figures had some propitiary symbolism and it became customary to bring them to a shrine as an offering.

Besides associations with everyday life, the view Hiroshige depicts could have had contemporaries recollecting classical literature. The key element here is the birds floating on the river.

They are *miyakodori*, "birds of the capital". The celebrated tenth-century novel *Ise monogatari* ("The Tale of Ise") tells of a courtier who flees from Edo and finds himself on the bank of the Sumidagawa. The courtier and his companions fall into despair at the thought of how far they have come.

At that point white birds with red beaks and feet, the size of snipes, flitted across the water. They asked their interpreter what they were and when he replied "birds of the capital", the courtier composed a verse:

If you are indeed
What your name purports, o "bird of the capital",
Then I should ask:
Is she still living
Who is in my thoughts?

This incident is held to have taken place near Hashiba-no watashi.

37. Tile Kilns by the Hashiba-no watashi Ferry on the Sumidagawa River

Sumidagawa Hashiba-no watashi kawaragama (4/1857)

Edo was created as a city for soldiers in service with the shogun or one of the *daimyo* whose duties included being present in the capital for a strictly fixed period. Each of them had an urban estate on which they lived with their large retinues. The samurai of the escort dispersed in lodgings throughout the city and found themselves cut off from their families for long stretches of time. There were always considerably more men in Edo than women. Even in the mid-eighteenth century there were two males for one female and relative parity took another hundred years or so.

At the start of the Edo period, the Eastern Capital was a "masculine city", its population made up of warriors and burghers – merchants, craftsmen and those who served them. This all created a favourable climate for ladies of easy virtue and that aspect of life could have got out of control, threatening the state policy of strict control in all spheres. In 1617 the government closed all "pleasure establishments", except those contained in special quarters controlled by the municipal authorities, which were called Yoshiwara.

Originally, this name was transcribed with the characters for "Reed Plain", since the quarters were built in an area where reeds grew thickly. Almost immediately, though, the first character "reed" was replaced by that for "happiness", which is pronounced the same. And so the "green quarters" came to be situated on the Plain of Happiness.

Buildings were put up forming five streets, enclosed on all sides by a ditch and fence, which clearly pointed to the extraordinary nature of the place.

The city grew, however, and by the middle of the seventeenth century, the "pleasure districts " were in the very centre, which ran contrary to the idea of isolating the dwelling places of courtesans. Moreover, they suffered from frequent fires. In the first half of the seventeeth century the quarters burnt at least four times.

The idea of shifting them had matured by the early 1650s and the legendary fire of 1657, which razed the areas by the Nihonbashi to the ground, provided the final impetus. In 1657 they moved to a new site, by the Nihon-zutsumi dyke in the Asakusa district, which became known as Shin- ("New") Yoshiwara. Here the quarters began to flourish. The population grew rapidly and now occupied seven streets. By the time the series was produced, Yoshiwara was considered the most interesting, luxurious and expensive area of its kind in Japan.

Its streets, especially Nakanocho, the Central Avenue, were lined with many teahouses and shops selling a variety of goods, including special hats (*amigasa*) for those who wanted to keep their visit a secret. It was always busy here, except for the time before dawn when those who had stayed the night left Yoshiwara as the rules dictated.

That early hour is what Hiroshige chose for his print. The lanterns are still burning, but the horizon is already brightening and the sun will come up at any moment. A few people are about. Their faces are half-hidden by *hokammuri-zukin* ("cheek-covering hoods"), one of the means of remaining incognito. The visitors are being seen off by sleepy serving-girls carrying lanterns and the courtesans who by custom went with them as far as the Omon Gate, the main entrance to Yoshiwara.

The parting guests have cloaks (*haori*) thrown over their kimonos. Early spring mornings were chilly, and that is the time of year Hiroshige depicted, judging by the cherry trees in full blossom, which appear in the half-light of the foreground. These trees were a particular feature of Yoshiwara. They were planted out in specially prepared lawns only for the brief flowering season in early spring and then removed. The cherry blossom which begins to tumble from one branch before others have fully opened was in itself a symbol of the transience of life. In the "pleasure districts", this melancholy symbol became even more specific: pleasure is fleeting on the Plain of Happiness; everything comes to an end and eventually one has to leave Yoshiwara.

38. Dawn in the "Green Quarters"

Kakuchu shinonome (4/1857)

The main feature of this print is Kinryuzan, literally "the Mountain of the Golden Dragon" – the "mountain name" (*zango*) of the Sensoji Monastery. All monasteries had *zango*, something apparently connected with the fact that at one time Buddhist holy places were located in the mountains and took their names from them.

Sensoji was an old monastery, founded in the reign of the Empress Suiko (592-628). According to legend two brothers fishing in the lower Sumidagawa found a small gilded Buddhist statuette in their net. They threw it back into the water, but when they next drew up their net it was there again. The brothers then presented the little figure to their overlord who installed it respectfully in his palace. Later a special temple was built for the statuette.

In the year of his death, Ennin (794-864), one of the most prominent leaders of the Tendai school, visited the monastery. On his orders a new temple was constructed and since then the monastery adhered to the Tendai school. It had its heyday under the Tokugawa dynasty, when Edo became the capital of Japan.

In 1618, two years after Ieyasu's death, the first Toshogu (mausoleum of Ieyasu) was built here. It did not exist for long, however: in 1642 it was destroyed by fire and reconstructed on a new site.

In Hiroshige's time the monastery had two pagodas, one with five tiers, the other with three, a main temple (*hondo*), a "thunder gate" (*kaminari-no mon*), a hexagonal temple (*rokkakudo*) and other buildings. Hiroshige recorded their appearance from different points of view in several prints of the series. Here the red five-tier pagoda and massive hondo can be seen in the middle distance on the right.

Sensoji was the centre of Asakusa, a distinctive district which formed the northern outskirts of the capital. In Hiroshige's day it was the location of three Edo *Kabuki* theatres, the home of writers and artists, particularly those whose work and attitudes differed from those generally accepted.

From the late 1650s, the district had included Yoshiwara, Japan's most significant "green quarter".

The foreground of the print is occupied by part of a *yanebune* (or *yakatabune*), a covered pleasure boat. Passengers were entertained by geishas who served them wine and food, and performed songs to the accompaniment of the *shamisen*. The presence of people in the scene is barely indicated: the figure of one of the geishas (there should have been at least two) is abruptly cut off by the left-hand edge. The boat is heading across the Sumidagawa to the mouth of the Sanyabori Canal which led to Yoshiwara.

The starting point for the yanebune was Mukojima, on the bank of the Sumidagawa. At one time Mukojima was an area of vegetable plots and paddies. It was also a centre for falconry, which almost all the Tokugawa shoguns enjoyed. Gradually ordinary citizens began to spend their leisure time in Mukojima too. Shogun Yoshimune planted cherry-trees here and it became a favourite place to admire the blossom (and still is today). Mukojima was also noted for its holy places, above all Mimeguri-jinja, a Shinto shrine to the harvest deity Inari.

Mimeguri means "three circuits". There is a legend that during its construction a monk dug up a jug containing a sculpture of Inari in the guise of an old man. At that moment a white fox, the messenger of the deity, appeared from nowhere, ran three times around the sculpture, and equally mysteriously disappeared.

The shrine was also a centre of the cult of the seven gods of happiness (*shichifukujin*), the most popular figures in Japanese beliefs. Each of them granted a "happiness": wealth, lack of care, longevity, a successful career.

Nonetheless, it was the cherry orchards that really drew people to Mukojima and Mimeguri-jinja in particular.

The party in the boat appears to have just been admiring the blossom. Petals fly across the river as if following the boat.

39. Distant View of the Kinryuzan and the Azumabashi Bridge

Azumabashi Kinryuzan enbo (8/1857)

The Kanda aqueduct was one of the largest canals supplying the capital with water for drinking and other purposes.

It began at the Inokashira-no ike pond (see No. 87) and then followed the course of the Kandagawa river eventually reaching the Sekiguchi dam.

The area was included in the city as the Sekiguchi-daimachi district in 1720. The great adornment of this suburb was Camellia Hill (Tsubakiyama), the slopes of which really were strewn with those flowers in the past. They were still there in the 1850s, although in Hiroshige's print the hill is only beautified by cherry trees in full bloom. "Omissions" of this kind, were probably prompted by compositional considerations: the bright flowers might have fragmented the powerful structure and strict rhythm of the work.

Another attraction of the district was the Suijinsha shrine on the top of the hill. It was dedicated to the water deity Mizuka-no me, who protected the water of the canal. In Hiroshige's print, the shrine is hidden in the dense grove visible in the upper right-hand corner.

The modest building lower down the slope is the Ryugean ("Retreat of the Dragon"), which belonged to a nearby Zen monastery. It became associated with Basho (1644-1694), one of the most famous Japanese poets, who lived here for a brief time in the 1670s while in the service of a *daimyo*. After his death, in the early years of the eighteenth century, his pupils raised a memorial mound close to the building, topped with a stele inscribed with one of his poems:
In a May downpour
Who will be able to take shelter
On the Setahashi bridge!

Somewhat later a memorial pavilion, Bashodo, was erected alongside.

In the print these structures cannot be seen, but Hiroshige managed to convey the spirit of poetry and the atmosphere of thoughtful contemplation, which marked both life in a Zen Buddhist monastery and Basho's verse, with a subtlety characteristic of his finest works.

40. The Bashoan Retreat on Tsubakiyama near the Aqueduct in the Sekiguchi Quarter

Sekiguchi jôsuibata Bashôan Tsubakiyama (4/1857)

In this print we find ourselves back near the shogun's castle on the bank of the Sotobori, the "External Moat" that cut right across the city (see No. 85). The area around the castle was for the most part occupied by the mansions of major feudal lords. At the upper left, we can see the fire-watchtower and wall of an estate belonging to the Owari clan, a side-branch of the ruling house.

Close by were the residences of two other side-branches of the Tokugawa house: Mito and Kii (see No. 54). Originally these were located within the castle, but after the tremendous fire of 1657 that destroyed almost all the buildings inside the fortified walls, they were moved to the area between the castle and the Sotobori.

The place-name Ichigaya literally means "Market Valley". Its origin is obscure, but it is possible that at some time there really was a market here.

Ichigaya's many teahouses were known throughout the country for their women of easy virtue. The awning of one teahouse can be seen on the left.

The composition is dominated by an ensemble, which in reality was not so grand – the Hachiman-jinja, one of the oldest Shinto shrines in Edo. It was founded in the fifteenth century, but soon destroyed by war and restored by Tokugawa Ieyasu. The shrine, dedicated to Hachiman, the Shinto god of war and the most powerful protector of Buddhism, was noted in Hiroshige's day for its bells.

It contained one of the nine bell-towers set up by the municipal authorities to ring the hours.

The main attraction of the shrine was, however, an open-air stage for ritual Shintoist dances (*kagura*). Its presence is indicated in the print by another tea pavilion. Decorated with red paper lanterns, it lies directly beneath the building of the shrine, on the path leading to the stage.

This print differs from the majority of the series: the composition is more fragmented and at the same time unprepossessing; the strip of stylized clouds is clumsily used and looks forced, and so on. This is one of three prints attributed to Hiroshige II, a pupil of Hiroshige, who was also known as Shigenobu. All three were published after the master's death, in the Tenth Month of 1858 and display a different style of signature. Nevertheless, it is not clear whether these works were wholly created by Hiroshige II or produced from sketches left by Hiroshige.

41. The Hachiman Shrine in Ichigaya

Ichigaya Hachiman (10/1858)

This print takes us to the western fringes of the capital, to a district called Shinjuku located by the Tamagawa, a twenty-mile-long canal that supplied a considerable part of Edo with drinking water. In Hiroshige's day the banks of the canal were occupied by the properties of *daimyo*. On the left is the entrance to the mansion of the Naito clan, who played a major part in the formation of the district.

Originally the Naito estate covered the whole of Shinjuku, but later one of the family granted land here to six vassals. Six mansions appeared in this area, prompting the name Rokkenmachi ("the Six-House Quarter"). In the late seventeenth century a group of wealthy burghers applied for permission to build inns and amusement establishments here. The result was a new urban district, Naito-Shinjuku – "the New Houses on the Naito Estate".

This area lay on the Koshukaido highway, leading west to the mountainous regions of Honshu. In Shinjuku you could put up at an inn, hire or change horses, porters or palanquins at the post station, or drop into one of the eating-houses, where customers were served by women (*meshimori*), who were not adverse to offering more intimate services. Shops sprang up, as did shrines and monasteries. The district flourished for some twenty years, until a special government decree forbade all commercial activity in Shinjuku.

The reason was a clash between a commoner and a high-ranking samurai.

The samurai got into an unpleasant situation with a meshimori and was beaten up by the establishment's "bouncer". This was an insuperable blow to the family's honour. The samurai's elder brother made him commit *hara-kiri*. He then cut off his head and holding it appealed to the authorities, requesting that his clan be stripped of its allotment, but that Naito-Shinjuku should also be closed. The district only revived over fifty years later. In 1772 its rights were restored by Tanuma Okitsugu (1719-1788), a statesman fond of worldly pleasures.

Since then the popularity of Shinjuku's establishments grew enormously and their numbers increased apace.

The district developed into one of the busiest places in Edo. It lay at the edge of the Eastern Capital and was therefore eminently suited to different "open-air" amusements. This is, for example, obviously why the people Hiroshige places on the embankment have come here, including an obviously organized group of women carrying parasols.

One of the establishments that made Shinjuku popular is shown on the right bank of the canal. Through the open awnings we can see three meshimori in red costumes entertaining a guest.

名所江戸百景

玉川
堤の花

広重画

42. Cherry-Trees in Blossom
on the Tamagawa Embankment

Tamagawa zutsumi-no hana (2/1856)

Summer

The area around the Nihonbashi Bridge held a special attraction for all the inhabitants of Edo. It was the focal point of the daily activities of merchants and craftsmen, who gave rise to one of the most original phenomena in Japanese cultural life – *chonin-no bunka*, the culture of townspeople.

The Nihonbashi is easily recognized by the finials like tongues of flame on the posts of the railing. They were reserved for use on especially important bridges (see No. 76).

Between the Nihonbashi and Edobashi, there were markets on both sides of the river. The white-plastered warehouses in the upper part of the print were if not a sight, then a feature of the locality. Hiroshige chose to omit one of the main peculiarities of these buildings – the devices of the owners which were painted on them. There is a poem that goes:
If you cast a glance
From Edobashi, the barns stretch out
All covered with every manner of badge.

We are looking here at the south bank of the Nihonbashigawa, which was no less busy and commercial than Uogashi across the river. Wooden buildings extend along the bank, alternating with warehouses.

Aomono-ichiba, the Green (Vegetable) Market that began near the Nihonbashi, was the destination for most of the boats loaded with freight seen in the print.

The area immediately by the Edobashi was also known in the past for other businesses. There was a noted apothecary's, Mitsuhoshi ("Three Stars"), which specialized in plasters and ointments for various purposes.

Alongside it was Kinokuniya, one of the best tobacco shops in the city. The south bank between the two bridges was the venue for an annual event known as *saizo-ichi*. Saizo was the name given to the singers and actors who went from house to house giving small performances at the New Year. In the last ten days of the old year, actors from elsewhere (mainly neighbouring provinces) wishing to take part presented themselves at this "talent show" where they were selected and rates of pay decided.

The composition is based on a sharp juxtaposition of planes: we look at the river through the superstructure of the bridge. Closer, almost level with us, is a basket that is hanging from a yoke (we only see the ropes hanging from the crosspiece) carried by a fish-hawker. The basket contains *hatsugatsuo*, the "first mackerel".

Mackerel fishing began at the end of the Third Month or the beginning of the Fourth off the island of Enoshima. It was the first fish of the New Year to reach the market in Uogashi. There was a saying about the joys of spring: "Green foliage for the eyes; the mountain cuckoo for the ears; the first mackerel for the taste." *Hatsugatsuo* was incredibly expensive, yet there were ardent enthusiasts who would not even wait for the fish to reach the market and bought it straight from the boats. By Hiroshige's time, the prices for *hatsugatsuo* had come down, but it remained a luxury.

It was important to start trading as early as possible: less competition meant higher prices. Our unseen hawker is crossing the bridge in the cool of early morning, when the sun is just appearing above the horizon, as if justifying another interpretation of the name Nihonbashi – "the Bridge of the Source of the Sun".

43. The Nihonbashi and Edobashi Bridges

Nihonbashi Edobashi (12/1857)

The Nihonbashi district was a flourishing centre of trade and crafts. The samurai, the ruling military class, did not live here. It was the preserve of the merchant class, at least of its more successful, at times fabulously wealthy members. Suffice it to mention such businesses as Mitsubishi, Mitsui and Mitsukoshi, which are still "household names" today.

Nihonbashi was also noted as the focal point of Edo's distinctive urban culture, which gave the literary world Saikaku and Bakin, and the fine arts a whole galaxy of *ukiyo-e* artists.

In the Edo period commerce and culture were inseparably bound together: the brilliant flourishing of urban art would hardly have been possible without the patronage of the rich merchants.

All sorts of goods were sold in Nihonbashi. It was a centre of the timber trade, which, in a city where fires were a regular occurrence and wooden houses were continually being built or rebuilt, was a real "licence to print money". In general though, Nihonbashi specialized in the cloth trade. The majority of fabric shops belonged to men whose roots lay in the provinces of Omi and Ise. The shops were concentrated on First Street in the Nihonbashi district.

The shop in the print bears the trademark and name of Shirogiya, one of the leading fabric businesses. Founded in 1662 by a native of Omi, Shirogiya soon became a rival to Echigoya. It required a fair degree of inventiveness. Shirogiya's particular ploy was to send its salesmen out with small amounts of goods wrapped in a special shawl to different parts of the city, particularly to the mansions of the nobility who were its main customers.

After the Meiji revolution of 1868 Shirogiya became the first business to start trading in European-style fabrics for suits cut in the Western manner.

The firm still exists – as part of Tokyoan, one of the most extensive department-store chains in Japan. Further back in the print is an eating-house selling thin noodles made of buckwheat flour (*soba*). The white fabric awning above the entrance bears the characters of its name – Tokyoan.

The passers-by carry paper parasols as protection against the sun. On the right is a melon-trader's stand. A messenger from Tokyoan hurries past it carrying a tray with a box of *soba* and tableware: he is delivering lunch to one of the shops in First Street.

The group in the centre are performers whose speciality was the Dance of the Sumiyoshi Shrine, which invariably featured a large, two-tier parasol.

They are followed by a woman wearing a broad hat and cotton kimono who is holding a *shamisen*. Everything suggests that she is a wandering singer or story-teller (*onna-dayu*) who presented folktales (*gidayu-bushi*), popular songs and fragments of *Kabuki* plays to the accompaniment of the *shamisen*. *Onna-dayu* were categorically forbidden to wear silk clothing. But the profession did require a certain attractiveness and so street singers dressed in kimonos that were narrow down below and had a then-fashionable large pattern that showed off their shapes, and high wooden sandals (*geta*) which helped to create a slender figure.

This was one of the rich quarters of the Eastern Capital. Hiroshige depicted two-storey buildings with plastered walls painted black. Such houses were relatively fireproof and expensive, owned by the most wealthy residents of the city. The "black houses" formed a striking contrast with the barracks (*nagaya*) in which the majority of Edo's populace – both townspeople (*chonin*) and poor samurai – rented living space.

44. First Street in the Nihonbashi District

Nihonbashi tori Itchôme ryakuzu (8/1858)

Yatsumi-no hashi can be translated as "the Bridge of Eight Views": it affords attractive views in all directions. Hiroshige recorded one of them: a panorama of Edo Castle and the mansions of *daimyo* to its left crowned by the majesty of Mount Fuji. The name can also be understood as "a view of eight bridges". The 1829 work Gofunai biko ("Notes on the Capital") says "Yatsumi-no hashi got its name because from it one can see Gofukubashi, Kajibashi, Dosanbashi, Zenikamebashi, Nihonbashi, Edobashi and the little bridge beyond Zenikamebashi."

This crossing point where the canal leading to the castle joined the Nihonbashigawa was an unusual place in the Eastern Capital. It was surrounded by a variety of enterprises, workshops and shops, the majority of which belonged to the Goto family, who passed on from generation to generation the secrets of various crafts, most notably the art of making sword blades and other metal articles.

Like most of their fellows in the Edo period, the craftsmen here not only produced goods, but also sold them in shops adjacent to their workshops.

The bridge was a busy place and perhaps for that reason a notice-board giving information about missing children was set up at its southern end in 1857.

In the print the bridge is barely hinted at: we see only the upper part of the railing leading up to it. There is, however, a sensation of a large number of people in intensive motion. It is created by the parasols held by the invisible pedestrians pressing tightly together.

Across the Nihonbashigawa, where boats loaded with brushwood pass anchored fishing vessels casting distinctive square nets, we see another bridge – the Zenikamebashi. From the early days of Edo as the capital, this bridge was noted for the various monetary operations on offer nearby. The area around the Zenikamebashi remains the financial centre of Tokyo today.

45. Yatsumi Bridge

Yatsumi-no hashi (8/1856)

The area around the ferry was in no way remarkable, and can hardly have excited the interest of Hiroshige's contemporaries. The artist though drew no fundamental distinction between the public face and the back alleys of the Eastern Capital. The bustle and care of daily life was to be found here too, on this stretch of the Nihonbashi and in the twin quarters of Koamicho and Kayabacho that lined its banks. Both were inhabited by merchants and were active centres of trade.

We are standing on the Kayabacho side. Its name meaning "Miscanthus Stores" reflects the fact that in the early years miscanthus, reeds and other roofing materials were sold here. Warehouses and commercial premises stood along the river, while dwelling houses stood in the "inner" part of the quarter.

The speciality of Koamicho was wholesale trade. The white-walled warehouses that Hiroshige shows running in even rows to the horizon contained all manner of foodstuffs and other goods. This was also the location of a shipping company (*kaisen-monya*) providing passenger and freight transportation.

The greater part of the print is occupied by the busy river. In the distance are boats loaded with tea, as can be seen from the inscriptions on the bundles. On the Koamicho side vessels are waiting to be loaded. A man in a small boat (*chokibune*) hurries about his business. In the left foreground Hiroshige depicts the prow of a large freighter or fishing vessels (*godairiki*), which sailed the rivers and coastal waters.

We witness the scene as if through the eyes of the woman in the foreground with her back to us. She is dressed in an outfit with the kind of large pattern fashionable in the mid-nineteenth century and is making her way to the ferry terminal in Kayabacho. The ferry itself, visible on the left of the print, is a relatively small vessel crammed with passengers who are forced to make the crossing standing up.

The name Yoroi-no watashi, the "Armour Ferry", comes from a tale associated with Minamoto Yoshiie (1041-1108), a rebellious warrior of the late Heian period who was famed not only for his valour and military skills, but also for his poetic abilities. The story goes that while he was crossing to the coast of Shimosa province, a storm blew up and his overloaded boat threatened to sink. Yoshiie threw his armour overboard as a sacrifice to the dragon that ruled the watery element and was saved.

46. The Yoroi-no watashi Ferry to the Koamicho Quarter

Yoroi-no watashi Koamichô (10/1857)

This was the most "Chinese" place in the Japanese capital. The bridge, the steep slope called Shoheizaka and the boundary wall of Seido were all connected with Confucius, the originator of the world's oldest state ideology, the father of the "Chinese tradition". The Kandagawa, seen here between steep green banks, was part of a large waterway, which began on the Musashi plain and flowed into the Sumidagawa. The bridge was built across it in the 1640s.

The "Shohei" element in the name of the bridge is the Japanese version of Qufu, the place in China where Confucius was born. The bridge had other names – Aioibashi, "the Bridge of Life (or Birth) Together", and Imoarai-bashi, "the Bridge Where Potatoes Are Washed", but the official and generally used name was Shoheibashi, which was taken to mean "the Bridge leading to the academy of the Shoheiko", which stood on the right bank of the Kandagawa. This complex, whose existence is only hinted at in the print, was constructed at the instigation of Shogun Tsunayoshi. In Hiroshige's time and long afterwards it shaped the character of the whole area. Confucianism was known in Japan at least from the seventh century, and in the Edo period it was adopted as the established state ideology and an official branch of learning.

In 1630 Shogun Iemitsu granted land on Shinobu-ga oka Hill (see No. 11), to Hayashi Razan (1583-1657), the leading Confucian scholar of the day who was in the service of several Tokugawa rulers, for him to build a mansion. In the grounds Razan established a library and a private school that later developed into a religious centre and a highly predigious educational establishment. The lectures given on various aspects of Confucian teaching were mainly attended by the children of *daimyo* and *hatamoto* over the age of twelve, although the classes were open to all, even peasants. All students took an examination, which was known as *sodoku-gimmi*, "the test of reading". To fail the test meant to lose many opportunities: a career in the service became impossible, nor could you become the head of a clan, or join another family as an adopted son.

The locality was quite a lively one like anywhere frequented by students. Hiroshige probably depicted some of them on the slope.

The barges are returning with loads of timber from the stores in nearby Yushima Yokocho.

For all the wealth of associations that Hiroshige's depiction of the locality evokes, the main element here is a complex interplay of rhythm and volumes.

As was frequently the case in the "pure landscape" works of the series, the real-life appearance of the place has been transformed by the artist, in the present case with the aim of creating an inwardly tense sense of movement in the print, as if reflecting the atmosphere of youth and diversity that reigned around "Edo's only university".

47. The Shoheibashi Bridge, the Temple of Confucius and the Kandagawa

Shôheibashi Seidô Kandagawa (9/1857)

Mount Fuji, the sacred symbol of Japan, could be seen from almost everywhere in old Edo, but the finest view was from Surugadai hill in the Kanda district. One of the works of the Edo period says: "When you contemplate the summit of Fuji from that spot, it seems you see it in the palm of your hand." A popular poem expressed the same idea in a different way:
There is an eminence in Edo,
It is like a pedestal
On which Fuji towers.

When Ieyasu set about organizing the new capital, the area below the hill was given over to housing for merchants and craftsmen, while mansions for the military class were erected on the hill. The name Surugadai arose because the *daimyo* of Suruga province was granted land on the hill.

The panoramic view of the mansions of "the shogun's immediate vassals" unfolds at the foot of Mount Fuji. The location of the residence of the *daimyo* of Suruga is clearly indicated by the fire-watchtower, a little black spot in the very centre of the print. Alongside lay the barracks of one of the ten government fire brigades. It is not, however, the watchtower, nor the sea of grey samurai mansions, nor even Fuji, that first catch the attention, but the flags of various colours and shapes flying above the city.

There are *fukinagashi*, a type of military standard consisting of a long pole with a semicircular wooden top from which long silk bands fluttered: the name itself means "[things] floating on the wind". In Hiroshige's print a *fukinagashi* of red silk forms the compositional centre of the whole work. There are also *nobori* – vertical banners of military origin, but in this case bearing propitiatory inscriptions or a depiction of Shoki, the tamer of demons and evil spirits. This image came from China and in the Tokugawa period became popular as a protection against the supernatural and also as a deliverer from all manner of ailments, particularly smallpox.

Finally there are banners in the form of gigantic carp (*koinobori*), one of which makes up the entire foreground of the print. Such banners were called May flags (*gogatsu-nobori*). They were an indispensable attribute of the Festival of the 1st Day of the Horse (*Tango-no sekku*), better known as the Festival of Boys.

The day was celebrated in every home where there was a boy over the age of seven. It began with the children visiting their teacher and congratulating him. This was followed by a bellicose amusement – the battle of the irises (*shobuuchi*). At home a special hill was constructed on which expensive warrior dolls were arranged, and various nobori were flown.

At the beginning of the Edo period the banners were painted in only three colours: yellow, blue and red, and only about fourteen inches square. The subjects were mainly of a martial nature: *Ishiyama Gentaro Fighting with a Tiger, Kintaro and Takenuki Goro*. Only in the second half of the eighteenth century did they become substantially larger and more colourful. That period also saw the appearance of carp-banners.

The carp depicted in this way were called *shusse-no uo*, "the fish of success", an ancient and lofty symbol. In both China and Japan, the carp was considered the only fish capable of climbing a waterfall on its way upstream, after which, according to legend, it turned into a dragon.

48. The Suidobashi Bridge and Surugadai

Sudoibashi Surugadai (5/1857)

Oji remained on the outskirts of the city until the early twentieth century and was more rural than urban. Carefully delineated rice paddies set the keynote in its appearance. The quiet seclusion here was disrupted twice a year: in spring when the cherry trees blossomed and in autumn when the maple leaves turned a variety of colours.

Oji became widely known in the first decades of the nineteenth century with the flourishing of its Shinto shrine to the harvest god, Oji Inari-jinja. On the Day of the Horse in the Second Month of each year, when the kite festival (*Tako-matsuri*) was celebrated, kites of many different sorts were sold in the temple precincts and kite fights were held.

The Oji-gongen shrine was constructed in 1634 on the orders of the third shogun, and a century later the eighth shogun had cherry trees planted in the grounds, which made it famous.

The temple was noted for its main festival, celebrated on the 13th day of the Seventh Month. It was called the Feast of the Spears (*yari-matsuri*). It was accompanied by theatrical performances at which ancient dances (*dengaku*) were performed.

Then came the main event: the visitors threw hats trimmed with flowers (*hanagasa*) at each other. This turned into something like a battle, which accounts for the alternative name – the Festival of Disputes (*kenka-matsuri*).

Pilgrims were also attracted by the large number of natural cascades in the area of the shrines on Mount Asuka, the celebrated "Seven Waterfalls of Oji". The most popular of them was named in honour of Fudo, a protective deity that cleared evil spirits and all sorts of obstacles from the path of believers with fire and the sword.

In the popular mind, Fudo's functions became more specific. He turned into a defender from fires, a patron god of trade and a healer god, particularly efficacious for eye ailments. It became customary to perform ritual ablutions in the relatively small waterfall dedicated to the deity.

In Hiroshige's work this waterfall acquired enormous proportions; the human figures below seem small and insignificant in comparison. The irresistible rush of water should probably be seen as an expression of the might of Fudo.

49. The Fudo Waterfall, Oji
Oji Fudo-no taki (9/1858)

In the Edo period the village of Tsunohazu lay on the western outskirts of Edo, on the Koshukaido, one of the country's five great highways. In the nineteenth century it would have been wholly undistinguished, had it not been for the Kumano Junisha shrine, one of the oldest in Edo, which Hiroshige depicts in the bottom part of the print. Back in the early fifteenth century, long before the transfer of the capital, a certain Suzuki Kuro founded a daughter house of the Kumano-jinja shrine in Kii province. Junisha – "Twelve Shrines" – were needed for many deities displayed in the province of Kii and then transferred to Tsunohazu.

It was also known as Juniso, which, depending on the characters used to write it, could mean "Twelve Places", "Twelve Pairs" or simply "a large number". The shrine stood in a picturesque park, with an artificial pond, which takes up most of the print and a small waterfall that is not shown.

Junisha soon became surrounded by places of entertainment. Tea pavilions were set up on both sides of the pond and a large two-storey restaurant was also located in the immediate vicinity. The latter possibly belonged to the "amusement quarters" of Tsunohazu, the *karyukai* ("world of flowers and willows"), which also adjoined the pond.

50. The Kumano Junisha Shrine at Tsunohazu, Popularly Known as Juniso

Tsunohazu Kumano Junishâ zokushô Juniso (7/1856)

An intensification of censorship in literature and fine arts in the early 1840s resulted in the banning of several popular genres (the depiction of beautiful women and *Kabuki* actors). One of the means around such a ban was to use a landscape as a sort of screen. On the pretext of depicting the customs of some locality, legends or folk tales connected with it, artists and publishers managed to put out prints on forbidden subjects.

Sanno-matsuri was the main festival of the Hie-jinja Shinto shrine, located in the Kojimachi quarter (see No. 54) in the very centre of Tokyo. The shrine had a long history going back to ninth-century Kyoto. In the Edo period it became the family shrine of the Tokugawa line. If a boy was born into the family, the shogun would be duty-bound to make a pilgrimage and present an offering (in the form of a sword) to the temple. The festive procession dedicated to Oyamakuni-no kami, the deity of the shrine, had the special privilege of parading before the shogun and his kin within the castle.

The whole route from shrine to castle was strewn with fine pebbles and closed off by a low bamboo fence. Tall lanterns were set up along the way. They were also hung on the tops of the houses, which were decorated with artificial flowers and cloth hangings. Stages were built for dances and theatrical perfomances.

The festival took place every other year, between the 10th and 16th days of the Sixth Month, and was an enormously expensive display of opulence. Before 1841, the procession was prepared by 160 municipal quarters and included 57 *sansha*, literally "mountain chariots", floats decorated with patterned fabrics and topped with sculptures. Then laws against excessive luxury were introduced. The procession became more modest, but Sanno-matsuri remained (and still remains) one of the city's favourite festivals.

In Hiroshige's print the procession is moving towards the Hanzomon gate of the castle. The man who gave his name to the gate was Hattori Hanzo, the head of one of the most powerful clans of *ninja* – professional spies, whose mansion once stood nearby. At present he is enjoying new fame as the hero of Japanese television series.

The first *sansha* in the procession is that of the Minami-Demmacho quarter. It is crowned by the figure of a monkey dressed in formal costume (*kariginu*) and a gold-coloured ceremonial hat (*tori-eboshi*). It has a sword at its belt and a large *gohei* scroll in its hand. This was the "messenger" of Sanno, the deity of Hie-jinja.

Next came the float of the Odemmacho quarter (right in the foreground of the print), which was topped by the figure of a cockerel standing on a drum. This was originally a Chinese symbol. In Ancient China a special drum was set up at the entrance to state institutions, which anyone could use to warn the ruler of sedition or injustice. The practice was adopted in Japan in 645 and it even gave rise to a saying – "*kanko-o kakemusu*", "the drum is moss-covered", meaning that all was well in the country.

The arrangement of the floats in this order makes sense: both the monkey and the cockerel (or chicken) were among the junishi, the twelve animals indicating the year in the lesser cycle of the Far Eastern calendar. The Year of the Chicken came after the Year of the Monkey. But when the shogun himself was to view the procession, it was the cockerel that entered the castle first, possibly as a display of loyal appreciation of the wise shogun and his "unclouded" rule. Some researchers believe that this influenced the composition, that by placing the cockerel and drum in the foreground, Hiroshige was emphasizing, as it were, its pre-eminent role in the procession. This print serves as a direct sequel to Soto-Sakurada Benkeibori Kojimachi, which was produced (or at least published) three months later.

51. Sanno Festival Procession on First Street in the Kojimachi Quarter

Kojimachi-itchôme Sanno-matsuri nerikomi (7/1856)

Hiroshige places us on the south bank of the Tameike pond in centrally-located Akasaka between the large trees that gave the locality its name – Kiribatake, "the Plantation (Field) of Paulownias". These attractive trees of the figwort family were planted around the man-made pond in the early eighteenth century, but some hundred years later, in 1811, most of them were felled. Dwelling houses and leisure establishments appeared here.

The latter were noted for a dish of rice boiled with barley and flavoured with grated sweet potatoes, and also for their serving-girls who in the eighteenth century ousted the local courtesans (*furoya-yujo*) from the public bathhouses. Some of the paulownias survived into the 1850s, adorning the pond, which appeared as a result of a miscalculation during the construction of the Sotobori canal in the early seventeenth century. About the same time as the trees appeared, the pond was seeded with lotuses, and the flowers can be seen in the print, by the opposite bank. The construction of houses around the pond began to spoil the water. The banks grew marshy, the pond partially dried out and shrank, but, judging by the print, it retained its original gourd-like shape. The narrow neck runs away to the left, or north, where it overflows into the lower-lying channel of the Sotobori (see No. 113). The pond no longer exists: in 1910 it was filled in.

On the left (north-eastern) bank of the pond we can see some buildings with a pine grove behind. They belong to the Sanno-jinja, a shrine famous for its biennial procession.

52. The Plantation of Paulownias in Akasaka

Akasaka Kiribatake (4/1856)

The Zojoji monastery was the most important and influential centre of the Jodoshu (Pure Earth) school in Edo. It occupied an enormous area. Its annual income was roughly as much as that of some provinces and more than 3,000 novice monks were studying there at any one time. It owed its success to very close ties with the ruling dynasty, which began with its foundation by Tokugawa Ieyasu. In Hiroshige's series, Zojoji is depicted several times from different places and angles. Here we see the south-east part, the "backs" of the monastery complex and the five-tier pagoda (there was another with three tiers).

This pagoda was constructed by Sakai Uta-no kami Tadayo (1572-1636), the master of the Shirasagi ("White Heron") castle at Himeji and advisor (karo) to the second Tokugawa shogun, Hidetada (ruled 1605-1623), of whose mausoleum it forms a part. The pagoda belonged to a special temple outside the monastery precincts and stood in a dense grove. It is believed that the trees had a role in fire-protection. In Hiroshige's print only the upper two tiers of the pagoda rise above the foliage.

The Zojoji monastery grounds included a vast necropolis containing the tombs of members of the ruling house. The graves of the shoguns were evenly divided between Kanyeiji and Zojoji, each possessing six.

Zojoji is flanked on both sides by a "city of temples" as the earliest Western guidebooks described it. Each of the mausoleums was enclosed by a fence, while the path leading to their ornately carved gates, was lined by a host of bronze lamps, many of which were donations to the monastery.

From 1868, when Shogun rule ended, the monastery was dogged by misfortune. Buddhism ceased to be the state religion. Zojoji became impoverished. Many of the buildings were taken over for other purposes while the immense grounds were turned into Shiba Koen, one of the first public parks in Tokyo. The mausoleums gradually became predominantly tourist attractions. The tragic culmination came with the air raids of 1945.

In Hiroshige's print we see the Furukawa river that ran alongside the monastery complex. As so often with Edo's rivers, it had a local name here – the Akabanegawa. The whole area was known as Akabane and the bridge as the Akabanebashi.

A major sight of Akabane was the mansion that stood on the opposite bank from Zojoji. The red gate contrasting with the dull, monotone walls makes it stand out in the print. It belonged to a branch of the Arima family who came from Chikugo province (the north of Kyushu island). The mansion's fire-watchtower was the tallest in the capital at about thirty-three feet. A widely-told story claimed that at the top of this tower Otogawa Kisaburo (1758-1806), one of the most famous *sumo* warriors in history, fought with a man who transformed himself into a monstrous cat, and won.

The Arima estate was, however, most famous for Suitengu, the Shinto shrine, in its grounds. Six vertical banners rising from the band of stylized cloud indicate its position. Suitengu was built in 1818 as a daughter house of the long-established shrine on the Arima estate on Kyushu. It was particularly popular among women seeking to give birth without trouble.

The area between the pagoda and the mansion is almost deserted in the print, but on feast days, it was a very different matter. On the fifth of each month, when there was a fair, the bridge was all but impassible and people crowded in front of the stalls.

53. Pagoda of the Zojoji Monastery and Akabane

Zojôjito Akabane (1/1857)

Here again we are in the very centre of the city, close to the shogun's castle. Sakurada literally means "Cherry Field" and one of the works of the Tokugawa era states: "Rice paddies extend from the Toranomon gate (see No. 113) to the outskirts of Atago. On the boundaries between the fields there are cherry trees, numbering several hundred thousand." In the Eighth Month of 1590, when Tokugawa Ieyasu first inspected the site of his new capital, he was struck by this spectacle and gave orders for the trees to be transplanted to the castle precincts. With time the paddies disappeared too: they were replaced by the mansions of influential feudal lords and high-ranking samurai.

Sakurada was divided in two: Inner (*Uchi-*) and Outer (*Soto-*). Soto-Sakurada included a number of central quarters, notably Kojimachi.

Kojimachi is one of the most ancient places in the city. Here in 1877 Edward S. Morris excavated the first "shell mound", which, apart from the sea-shells indicating how the earliest inhabitants fed themselves, contained ceramics and sculpture of religious significance. The mound became known as Omori Kaizuka, but the name Kaizuka, meaning "shell mound", was being used as early as the fifteenth century for a place on the road, which ran along the sandbar before the capital was moved. The settlements that sprang up along that road were called Kojimachi. Monasteries appeared on the route, most notably Zojoji (see No. 53). This was the location of the mansions of the "loyal barons" (*fudai-daimyo*), first and foremost three clans related to the Tokugawa dynasty who took their names from the provinces that they administered: Owari, Kii and Mito.

Plots in Kojimachi were also granted to others who had been of particular assistance to Ieyasu in the power struggle, including the Ii family. Their mansion stood on a hill facing the Benkeibori, and its red southern (main) gate features prominently in the print.

The canal got its name from the owner of the plot – Benkei Kozaemon, a noted bridge-builder in the capital.

There are many landscapes in the series unenlivened by an urban crowd, but this particular print has a strange melancholy reverie, quiet and self-absorption about it. The rich and varied life of one of the world's greatest cities somehow stopped short of these green canal banks.

54. The Benkeibori Canal from Soto-Sakurada Looking Towards Kojimachi

Soto-Sakurada Benkeibori Kojimachi (5/1856)

Tsukudajima was one of two islands in the mouth of the Sumidagawa. It got its name in the early seventeenth century when Tokugawa Ieyasu issued a special decree moving thirty-three specialist *shirauo* fishermen here from the village of Tsukudamura (see No. 4).

The fishermen brought with them the cult of the deity of the Sumiyoshi shrine, the protector of seafarers. The shrine on Tsukudajima was noted for its *fujidana*, a kind of pergola entwined with wistaria (*fuji*), which bloomed in May. Admiring the violet flowers of the wistaria remains a traditional passion with the Japanese.

The shrine's real fame was, however, founded on its temple festival – Sumiyoshi-matsuri. Once every three years, on the 6th day of the Eighth Month, the immense head of a fantastic lion (*shishi*) and several palanquins (*mikoshi*) were solemnly paraded.

The sacred palanquins were dipped in the sea, symbolizing union with the sea deity that protected Edo Bay and those who sailed it. To the right of the festive banner we can see part of a lantern on the roof of the shrine. It is decorated with a *mitsutomoe* ornament (in the form of three commas) which represents the unity of Sky, Earth and Man. Behind the banner a sacred palanquin is being carried in procession to the sea.

Beyond, we have a panoramic view of Edo Bay and the opposite shore, at that time divided between the provinces of Awa and Kazusa. This view constantly drew artists and poets. For example, *Haifu yanagitaru* ("A Barrel of Haiku Verse"), an anthology of works from the late eighteenth and early nineteenth centuries, contains the following *senryu*:

Glance through the pine-branches
And you'll see two lands:
Awa and Kazusa.

55. The Sumiyoshi Shrine Festival on Tsukudajima

Tsukudajima Sumiyoshi-no matsuri (7/1857)

Although Fukagawa translates as "Deep River", it is actually the name of a place in south-eastern Edo. It came from Fukagawa Hachiroemon, a native of Ise province, who became the first to settle here in the Keicho era. Fukagawa lay on the far bank of the Sumidagawa and, although by the early nineteenth century it had become a densely populated area, it was still considered one of the outskirts.

This remoteness had its advantages. Up until the late 1710s, Fukagawa did not come under the Edo municipal authorities, and was not therefore so affected by the many strict regulations and bans operating in the capital. It became the home of beautiful courtesans whose only rivals were in Yoshiwara, the sole "green quarter" officially tolerated in Edo.

Without such approval, Fukagawa's "pleasure districts" were almost illegal, and the prices were appreciably lower than in Yoshiwara. A trip to Fukagawa became a favourite leisure activity for the inhabitants of the city centre, without necessarily being connected with sexual adventures.

Fukagawa had an established reputation as a place to catch fish and had celebrated seafood restaurants. It was also a popular destination with toxophilites. The Shinto temple Tomioka Hachimangu included a building where archery competitions were held in a 72-yard corridor.

Finally, an enormous attraction was the Gohyakurakanji monastery – the strangest place in the Eastern Capital, according to Kikuoka Mitsuyuki, a writer of the first half of the eighteenth century.

Where the Onagigawa canal joins the Sumidagawa, there is a bridge called Mannenbashi. *Mannen*, literally "a hundred thousand years", was an expression meaning longevity. How it became attached to the bridge is not known.

On the 15th day of the Eighth Month, the whole of Japan observed *hojoe*, the festival when birds, fish and turtles were released from captivity. Although Buddhist in origin, the festival was also celebrated at Shinto shrines, including Tomioka Hachimangu in Fukagawa. The inhabitants of Edo preferred for the ceremony sparrows and eels. Birds could be bought everywhere; fish and turtles were sold close to water, by the Mannenbashi, among other places. There was a certain logic to this: the turtle too was a long-established symbol of longevity.

The figure of the turtle placed in the foreground makes a sharp contrast with the idyllic riverscape. The impression is of being inside the picture, on a level with the turtle hanging from a beam of the bridge. Yet the composition is stable and balanced, imbued with that inner peace and harmony which is inherent in Hiroshige's most characteristic landscapes.

56. The Mannenbashi Bridge in Fukagawa

Fukagawa Mannenbashi (11/1857)

Moving down the Sumidagawa, the main river of the Eastern Capital, Hiroshige is gradually bringing us to its mouth. Here, close to the Mannenbashi bridge (see No. 56), a channel called the Hakozakigawa runs off the main river (known here as the Okawa) towards Mount Fuji. The colouring of the mountain is unusual: a black summit and white slopes.

The meeting of the two arms of the river forms an island enclosed by a fence, the location of fortified *daimyo* mansions. The place was called Mitsumata, meaning "a fork [in the river]". Another name is included in the title of the print. The section about Mitsumata in *Edo meisho zue* states: "This locality is called Wakarenofuchi, because here the streams of fresh and sea water divide." At high tide, then, the salt water of Edo Bay would come up river as far as here. The view depicted in the print would seem to be in line with the rest of the series. The strange thing is that the "sight" in this area no longer existed.

It had been Nakazu, a piece of reclaimed land created by infilling in 1771. Within five years it became perhaps the most popular entertainment district in Edo. Hannichi kanwa ("Idle Conversations for Half a Day"), one of the works devoted to the history of urban life in the city, has the following in the chapter devoted to the Sixth Month of the Fifth Year of Anyei: "This summer Mitsumata, the 'new land' created in the Ohashi, attained an unprecedented fame. Teahouses and various spectacles are flourishing here." It did not last very long, however.

In 1789, a government decree aimed at the "correction of morals" ordered Nakazu razed and it returned to being a sandbar in the bend of the river. The place lived on in popular memory, though, and the artist himself referred to it in a book published in 1850. The rough location of Nakazu is indicated in Hiroshige's print by the sailing-boat in the foreground.

57. Channels at Mitsumata Wakarenofuchi

Mitsumata Wakarenofuchi (2/1857)

The bridge shown here was built in 1693 by Shogun Tokugawa Tsunayoshi (1646-1709) to link the Nihonbashi district, the established centre of the city, with Fukagawa. It was remarkable for its size, but since the Ryogokubashi, the next bridge up the Sumidagawa (see No. 59), was then called Ohashi (the "Great Bridge"), this one acquired the name Shin-Ohashi – the "New Great Bridge".

The new bridge did make it easier to get about the city, a fact noted, for example, in verse by the celebrated poet Matsuo Basho (1644-1694), who lived in a modest dwelling on the riverbank in Fukagawa, east of the Shin-Ohashi.

The bridge was however prey to fires and floods. In the first fifty years of its existence it was repaired twenty times and became such a burden on municipal funds that the authorities decided to pull it down. The inhabitants of the quarters adjacent to the Shin-Ohashi objected and in 1744 they assumed financial responsibility for the bridge, receiving in return the right to charge a toll. In 1809 this responsibility was taken over by the Hishigaki shipping company and consequently it obtained monopoly rights over its exploitation.

The Atake in the title was the popular name for the far bank in Hiroshige's print. It came from the Atake-maru, one of the large naval galleys (*atake-fune*), which first appeared in the second half of the sixteenth century. This particular vessel was built in 1635 and for almost fifty years moored in this area.

Hiroshige depicted the Shin-Ohashi in a typical heavy summer shower. Such downpours were called *yudachi* – "evening appearances", as it was believed that Raijin, the thunder god brought them with him when he appeared on the Earth. At the end of the day black clouds suddenly gather and a powerful wind blows up. The heavens open, but the shower never lasts long and the sky soon clears. The people caught on the bridge hide themselves under broad-brimmed hats and straw capes as they dash to reach shelter.

58. A Sudden Shower
on the Ohashi Bridge and Atake

Ohashi Atake-no yudachi (9/1857)

The Ryogokubashi was one of the main bridges of the Eastern Capital. It was constructed immediately after the devastating fire of 1657 in order to link the already overpopulated part of the city with the eastern bank of the Sumidagawa. Officially known as Ohashi, the "Great Bridge", it became known to the citizens almost at once as Ryogokubashi – the "Two Provinces Bridge", as at that time the Sumidagawa was the boundary between Musashi province on the west and Shimosa on the east. The bridge became a centre of amusements, the most lively in the capital. The numerous teahouses and restaurants by the bridge were never quiet, day or night. But things came to fever pitch during the *kawabiraki* – the "opening of the river", the main summertime festival connected with the Sumidagawa (see No. 98).

In the print Hiroshige depicts an everyday scene with the usual bustle: freighters and passenger boats plying the river. On the closer western bank there is a row of tea pavilions. Small theatres, archery stands, restaurants and various sideshows remain behind the viewer's back, on the open area at the end of the bridge.

By the far bank we see a number of piles driven into the riverbed. This spot was known as Hyappongi, "A Hundred Piers". At one time the large quantity of piles here served as a sort of breakwater, preventing the bank being washed away by the strong current on the bend. Later, in the 1850s, the bank was reinforced with the masonry that can be seen in the print. Eighteenth and nineteenth-century guidebooks mention Hyappongi as an excellent place for anglers.

From close to the breakwater it was possible to cross to Asakusa on the Fujimi-no watashi, "the Contemplation of Fuji Ferry". In the western direction the boat out in the river afforded a fine view of the sacred mountain.

59. The Ryogokubashi Bridge and Okawabata Bank

Ryogokubashi Okawabata (8/1856)

The title here includes three names all used for the lower reaches of the River Arakawa: Asakusagawa, Okawa and Miyatogawa. We look at the bank as if from a bridge between the piers at the western end of the Ryogokubashi bridge.

Hiroshige has depicted one of the seasonal festivals – Oyama-mode, the pilgrimage to Mount Oyama. It fell in summer and lasted twenty days, from the 28th day of the Sixth Month. The purpose was to pray to the rain-deity (*amagoi-no kami*) that dwelt in the Afuri-jinja shrine on the top of the mountain.

The initial ceremony of ritual purification took place at the eastern end of the Ryogokubashi. The participants chanted a prayer to the god of the Afuri-jinja shrine, then each of them threw a dry rice stem into the river. If it was carried away by the current, that meant that the prayer had been heard; if it circled on the spot that it was a bad sign. Then the pilgrims set off for Oyama under the guidance of wandering Buddhist monks (*yamabushi*). One group of pilgrims is depicted in the centre of the print,

in a boat with a monk at the prow. He is blowing a large seashell, an attribute of a *yamabushi*. In the foreground we see a fragment of another boat.

In Henry Smith II's opinion, the men in it are craftsmen who have decided only to go as far as Ryogokubashi and not make the ascent of Oyama. As far back as 1758, a work, *Guchishui monogatari* ("A Collection of Bitter Complaints"), bemoaned the fact that for the young people of Edo the pilgrimage to Oyama had become simply an excuse to have a good time. These "pilgrims" will probably return to the city after the ceremony and parade through the streets handing out the *gohei* (ritual paper strips) stuck into a bundle of straw attached to a *bonten*.

The use of the *bonten* (a decorated pole) was borrowed from the religious practices of the *yamabushi*, which combined Buddhist and Shinto elements as well as certain elements of Chinese Taoist teaching. Both boats are heading for the jetty by the Yanagibashi bridge (see No. 32), where the Kandagawa joins the Sumidagawa.

60. The Asakusagawa River, Okawabata Bank and Miyatogawa River

Asakusagawa Okawabata Miyatogawa (7/1857)

Famous pine trees stood in many parts of the Eastern Capital. The Shubi-no Matsu ("Successful Conclusion") was noted for having a shape like a dragon. Its branches spread far out and hung over the Sumidagawa.

The original tree was broken by a hurricane in the Anyei era (1772-1780) and replaced by another, a process that was repeated several times. The tree grew between the Fourth and Fifth Moats enclosing the government rice stores. Its unusual shape was easily spotted from the river and soon it became one of the city's landmarks.

The strange name comes from a practice that became an engrained custom with visitors to the "green quarters" of Yoshiwara – to stop by the pine on the way back in the morning and relate the events of the night to each other from start to finish.

Of all the named pines, Shubi-no matsu was the one most often depicted in engravings, and it is also mentioned in poetry.

Hiroshige merely "indicates" a sight familiar to all and its immediate vicinity - a passenger in a *chokibune*. Since the stars are still out, he must be on his way to Yoshiwara. It is, however, not only the *chokibune* with its passenger intent on a night of pleasure and the pine that has heard tales of so many such nights, that would remind the contemporary viewer of the frivolous delights of life.

The boat whose prow features so prominently in the foreground is a *yanebune*, intended for banquets and more intimate amusements. The boat has pulled into the bank, the boatman cannot be seen and high-soled sandals (*geta*) have been discarded on the deck. Their owners are inside, behind the green cane blinds.

61. The "Shubi-no matsu Pine" and the Ommayagashi Bank on the Asakusagawa River

Asakusagawa Shubi-no matsu Ommayagashi (8/1856)

In his summer views Hiroshige does not stray far from the Sumidagawa, the main waterway in the city and a source of refreshing coolness.

Here we are in the precincts of the Komakatado Buddhist temple. It was built in the mid seventeenth century, burnt down in 1690 and was restored two years later. By the middle of the eighteenth century, it had acquired the location and appearance recorded by Hiroshige. As so often the artist gives us a fragmentary view: the lower left-hand corner is occupied by the curving roof and white-plastered walls.

A bronze statue of the bodhisattva Kannon, the Bringer of Children, stood in front of the Komakatado. The whole temple was dedicated to Kannon and its main sacred image was a sculptural depiction of the same bodhisattva in the form of Bato-Kannon (Hayagriva). That particular variant has a horse's head, which probably prompted the name of the temple (komakata means "in the form of a foal"). The temple was surrounded by various shops, leisure establishments and restaurants whose speciality was "violet carp".

The red flag on a long pole that forms an abrupt vertical element in the composition marks the Hyakusuke perfume shop which stood to the west of the temple. The red colour, symbolizing rouge, was conventionally used to indicate such businesses.

The flag is being pulled by the wind and beaten by the slanting raindrops. This view is of the summer rainy season (June and early July).

In the distance we are looking at the Honjo district and the Azumabashi dating from 1774 (see No. 39), one of the four major bridges over the Sumidagawa. A bird hangs in the stormy sky above Komakatado. Its appearance in this print is apt: the *hototogisu* cuckoo was associated with summer in Japanese poetry, representing a traditional image of the season.

But the temple also had its own, particularly strong ties with the *hototogisu* in the story of the love between Prince Sendai Date Tsunamune (1567-1636) and Takao, a celebrated courtesan. Their liason ended tragically: Takao was slain and Tsunamune forced to withdraw into a monastery. This story became widely known on account of a *Kabuki* play first performed in 1777. A poem by Takao, written in keeping with custom after her lover had left Yoshiwara to return to the city, goes:

Where art thou now?
Near Komakata.
The cuckoo's lament.

The name of the temple suggests the piercing call of the *hototogisu*. The bird introduces another range of associations into this complex depiction of a locality.

62. The Komakatado Temple and the Azumabashi Bridge

Komakatado Azumabashi (1/1857)

Here we are standing on the west bank of the Sumidagawa, looking at the part of the river where it is joined by the Ayasegawa. The banks of that tributary were noted for their rural delights. People went there to admire the flowers and listen to the chirping of the cicadas.

There is a story attached to this stretch of water that explains its rather strange name – Kanegafuchi, the "Bell Deep". In the mid-eighteenth century a bell cast in 1735 was being transported by boat from the Choshoji monastery to Hashiba (see No. 37) on the opposite bank. In the middle of the river the boat turned over and the bell sank. All attempts to raise it proved futile and the spot became known as the "Bell Deep".

This part of the Sumidagawa was considered to have particularly attractive mulberry trees and Hiroshige uses one of them, with pink flowers, as a "side-flap" for the scene he presents.

63. The Ayasegawa River and Kanegafuchi

Ayasegawa Kanegafuchi (7/1857)

This print is among the "decorative" works of the series – the exquisite lines of the flowers create a sort of ornamental effect. Nevertheless, this is a depiction of an actual locality. The artist has, as it were, crossed the Sumidagawa and turned eastwards, following the Ayasegawa about a mile and a half upstream to the village of Horikiri.

In the Edo period rice was grown here, but also flowers, including irises, that were sold at the capital's markets. This industry was recorded back in the 1660s, but its heyday came 150 years later, when a Horikiri peasant named Kodaka Izaemon and his son created a plantation where they grew various kinds of iris. Eventually Kodaka's garden contained about 6,000 plants representing 130 different varieties and it became an attraction for Edoans in the flowering season.

The visitors placed in the middle ground of the print are not obvious at first because of the huge flowers depicted almost natural size. They belong to the variety called *hanashobu* (iris kaempferi), which literally means "flowering sweet flag", a name, which arose because of the visual similarity between two plants. The sweet flag (*shobu*) was also grown at Horikiri and sold at the markets. Its leaves were used to scent bathwater and as a flavouring for *sake*. Sometimes they were fastened to the tops of houses to repel evil spirits.

The sweet flag was particularly in demand on the 5th day of the Fifth Month, the Festival of Boys (see No. 48) of which it punningly became an important symbol. Another word *shobu* meant "revering martial valour", which was a natural thing to wish the young heroes of the occasion.

The vogue for *hanashobu* had reached its height when Hiroshige made this print. About that time the flower became widely known in Europe, where large plantations were established.

The flower also had a certain influence on the fine arts, notably becoming one of the characteristic motifs of the *art nouveau*, a movement that absorbed many elements of Japanese artistic tradition.

64. Irises at Horikiri

Horikiri-no hanashôbu (i5/1857)

The foreground in this print consists exclusively of flowering wistaria (*fuji*), a symbol of summer. The Shinto shrine at Kameido was famous for its display of these blooms.

The shrine was dedicated to Sugawara Michizane (845-903), a minister and poet of the Heian period, who was deified after his death as patron of scholars and students, and also a thunder-god. Michizane died in exile far from the capital. He was buried at Dazaifu, close to the city of Fukuoka on Kyushu island and the main shrine to him is located there.

According to the legend, in 1662 a priest at Dazaifu had a prophetic dream. He took parts of a plum tree that grew at Dazaifu and Michizane himself had praised in verse, carved an image of Michizane in the village of Kameido near Edo and set up a small prayer-house (*hokora*) there. After the great fire of 1657, settlement of the east bank of the Sumidagawa began in earnest.

The undertaking was directed by Shogun Ietsuna (1641-1680), a zealous adherent of the Michizane cult. He interested himself in the modest prayer-house and soon (in 1663) a proper shrine dedicated to Tenjin-sama appeared at Kameido.

Ietsuna intended the shrine as protection from the north-west, where the kingdom of demons lay. The construction of the ensemble in the "image and likeness" of the main shrine at Dazaifu was supervised by two of the shogun's close associates.

The shrine was noted for its garden, a pond in the shape of the character *kokoro* ("heart", "soul") and two bridges indicating the way to Shinden. Such high-arched bridges are known as *taikobashi* – "drum bridges". One of them here was made of stone, the other of wood. The wooden bridge was considered "male", because it was larger; the masonry one, that came after it, "female". The print shows the former, but, it should be said, its height is somewhat exaggerated.

65. In the Precincts of the Tenjin Shrine at Kameido

Kameido Tenjin keidai (7/1856)

The writer Kikuoka Mitsuyuki called this "the strangest place in Edo" in his *Edo-no sunago* ("Edo Gilding") published in 1732. The monastery was situated in the east of Honjo, a new district of the capital. Everything that did not conform, that was strange, unusual or exotic gravitated to the outskirts of the city. The immutable laws of everyday life did not apply here and, in Gohyakurakanji as in Yoshiwara, the result was a topsy-turvy world where the abnormal was the norm. As Thinon Screach aptly remarked: "Rakanji was for the spirit what Yoshiwara was for the body."

The monastery was founded in the second half of the seventeenth century, but its real rise began in 1696, when Shogun Tsunayoshi granted it land in Honjo. The monastery's holdings grew under the following shoguns, but it remained "a monastery in the fields", outside the city limits.

The monastery belonged to Obaku-shu, a tendency within Zen Buddhism that had come from China in the seventeenth century. In 1661 the first Obaku monastery was built at Uji, halfway between Kyoto and Nara, but by the end of the eighteenth century there were already more than four hundred monasteries belonging to the school all over Japan.

Gohyakurakanji, like other Obaku monasteries, was strange on account of its overtly Chinese appearance. The monks affected Chinese dress; the buildings were in the Chinese style; and services were held exclusively in Chinese.

The monastery became well known in the capital through the activities of a monk called Shoun. He met the first abbot of Gohyakurakanji in Kyoto and in 1675 became a monk and set off on a pilgrimage around the country. While travelling through the Yabakei mountains on Kyushu, he saw statues of the five hundred *rokan* (disciples of the Buddha) cut into the rock and he vowed to create something similar in Edo. He produced the first statue in the early 1680s, in time for the old abbot to see and approve it. By the year 1710 all 500 statues were complete. In the 1720s they were moved into a special temple and arranged in an unusual and fascinating order. The 500 *rokan* made the monastery famous far beyond the bounds of Edo.

Visitors to the temple first encountered statues of the chief deities (also by Shoun). The interior was designed in such a way that they found themselves "face to face" with each of the rokan. There were no barriers between them and the sacred images. The viewer was inside the sanctum, as it were. The statues were life-size and the faces, worked with an almost frightening verisimilitude, created a tremendous impression. This gave rise to a custom connected with the Confucian principle of filial respect. When a parent died, the bereaved person would come here, seek out among the 500 individual "portraits" the one most like the deceased and perform a ritual of remembrance before it.

Even more famous, however, was another part of the monastery – Sazaido, the "Spiral Temple" that became a symbol of the place. It was this that Hiroshige chose to depict.

The word *sazae* means a spiral seashell and the three-storey building contained a spiral staircase by which pilgrims made their way around. The temple contained a hundred statues of the bodhisattva Kannon, copies of images of the deity in various monasteries around Japan. Each storey symbolized a pilgrimage of many days to thirty-three Kannons in one of three regions of the country. To go through all three levels of Sazaido was therefore reckoned the equivalent of a pilgrimage around the temples dedicated to this bodhisattva all across Japan.

66. The "Spiral Temple"
in the Monastery of the Five Hundred Rohan

Gohyakurakanji Sazaido (8/1857)

For the nineteenth-century citizens of Edo, "sights" included architectural monuments, historical relics, popular festivals and ceremonies.

A particular place might have been famous for its ephemeral beauties: the full moon, cherry blossoms, summer flowers, and so on. Rare spectacles of a different order might also qualify, for example, the Chinese egrets (*karashirasage*) to be seen near the Sakasai-no watashi, a ferry across the Nakagawa.

The place shown here is close to the spot where the Tatekawa canal joins the Nakagawa. Travellers headed for, say Narita, had to use the ferry, which took its name from the village visible on the opposite bank.

67. Sakasai-no watashi Ferry

Sakasai-no watashi (2/1857)

Going by the title of the print, the place depicted should belong to the Shinto shrine Hachiman, but we are actually in the precincts of the Buddhist monastery Eitaiji, which was famed for its garden.

Each year, on the 21st day of the Third Month, an "Opening of the Mountain" ceremony (*yamabiraki*) was held here. Buddhist monasteries were conventionally called "mountains" and so the ceremony marked the opening of the monastery, or more precisely its garden, to the public. At the same time, it was a festival dedicated to Kobo-daishi (774-835), the founder of the Shingon school of esoteric Buddhism, to which Eitaiji belonged.

Hiroshige's "mistake" regarding the location is easily explained: Eitaiji and Fukagawa Hachiman were both situated on the artificial island called Eitaijima. The monastery garden was at the same time the garden of the shrine. Both had been founded by a Shingon monk, Chosei-shonin, in 1624. Chosei was the first abbot of Eitaiji and Fukagawa Hachiman and his successors also held both offices.

Hiroshige may have named Fukagawa Hachiman here for another reason. The print is dated to the Eighth Month, the 15th day of which was the main festival of that shrine. This event was popularly known as *nobori-matsuri* – "the Festival of the Flags".

Members of the community (*ujiko*) competed in creating impressive banners on tall poles and displaying them both at the shrine itself and in the streets of Fukagawa. They are not present in Hiroshige's print, yet it is possible that the artist was deliberately combining features of the locality, not only toponyms, but also significant times.

He shows plum trees in blossom and flowering azaleas, although that could not have been correct: the plum comes into blossom at the very start of spring, while the azalea blooms in summer. The plum trees are seasonally connected with the monastery festival, the azaleas with that of the shrine.

One more detail, the artificial Fuji in the depth of the picture, tends to suggest summer. This *fuji-zuka* was put up in 1820 and, like all similar structures in Edo, it was ascended in summer – at the start of the Sixth Month. The term *yamabiraki* was also used for the start of the "climbing season", which is probably why it appears in the title here.

The evidently deliberate confusion of times does not disrupt the compositional unity of the print. For the Western viewer the seasonal discrepancies simply go unnoticed, while the Japanese will easily recognize and "decipher" them.

68. The "Opening of the Mountain" at the Fukagawa Hachiman Shrine

Fukagawa Hachiman yamabiraki (8/1857)

Up until 1872 Fukagawa could boast a Buddhist temple of unusual shape and function. It was called *Sanjusangendo* – the Thirty-Three-Ken Temple. The *ken* was a measure of length slightly less than six feet, and the name is usually translated in that light. In reality, though, the number referred to the bays between the columns which were two ken wide and therefore the gallery was 130 yards long. This is the structure cutting diagonally across the page that Hiroshige places in the foreground.

The pre-history of the Sanjusangendo in Edo goes back to "Classical Antiquity", that is to say the Heian period (794-1185).

In an 1836 publication, Edo meisho zue, the story behind the appearance of this building is told in some detail: It is said that in the Kanyei era (1624-1644) a master archer originally from Bingo province who lived in Edo suggested constructing for archery training a Sanjusangendo in imitation of a building in Kyoto's the Rengeoin monastery. A plot of land was accordingly allocated in Asakusa. Donations for the construction were collected from all the samurai clans and master carpenters were hired. The raising of the building on that site was completed in the Eleventh Month of the Year of the Horse – the 9th Year of Kanyei [1642]. But in the Ninth Month of the Year of the Tiger, the 11th Year of Genroku [1698], it fell victim to the all-consuming flames and was reduced to ashes. After that [in 1701], it was moved to the present site."

The prototype in Kyoto had been built back in 1164, on the orders of Emperor Go-Shirakawa (1127-1192). It contained 1001 wooden statues of the bodhisattva Senju-Kannon (the Thousand-Armed Avalokiteshvara). A very long hall was required to accommodate such a quantity of sculpture, hence the size and the popular name of the building. A gallery ran along its west wall which came to be used for an unusual kind of archery competition. These events quickly became famous and this prompted the appearance of a "twin" of the Kyoto temple in the early years of the Eastern Capital.

Overall the two are identical apart from a negligible difference in size and the decoration of the interior: the Edo temple contained only one statue of Senju-Kannon. As we have seen above, the Edo temple was from the start intended chiefly as a place for archery competitions.

These events demanded more than just accuracy. The distance to the target and the long, narrow corridor called above all for strength. The arrows had to fly straight and level in order not to hit the ceiling, so the archers fired from a sitting position. Yet the firing rate was also taken into consideration: the winner being the one who hit the target most times within a given period of time.

Competitions were held regularly and the results carefully recorded in a special journal which has come down to us today. The absolute record was established in 1838, by the eleven-year-old son of a samurai.

In ten hours he fired off 12,015 arrows (one every two seconds) of which 11,760 reached the target.

69. The Thirty-Three-Ken Temple in the Fukagawa District

Fukagawa Sanjûsangendo (8/1857)

In this area there were no famous temples or shrines, celebrated hot springs, cherry orchards or waterfalls to fire the imagination. This was an important junction in the complex system of waterways that linked all parts of the city.

Although the print is titled *The Mouth of the Nakagawa River*, in reality it shows the meeting-point of three of Edo's watery arteries: the Nakagawa, Onagigawa and Shinkawa.

The Nakagawa (literally "Intermediate River") was an arm of the Tonegawa, which flowed into Edo Bay. The name, according to one version, comes from the fact that it lies between the Tonegawa and the Sumidagawa. The river was noted as an excellent place to fish.

The first volume of *Ehon Edo miyage* ("A Picture-Book Souvenir of Edo"), an 1850s publication that Hiroshige illustrated, observes: "There are said to be many fish here. From the coming of spring until [deep into the] autumn boats are constantly scurrying about here, catching fish in nets and also with rods. It can be stated that many find pleasure at Nakagawa." Just above the centre of the print there are two boats with anglers in broad straw-hats.

In the Edo period the Nakagawa was used to transport salt, which was mined at Gyotoku by the mouth of the Edogawa. In all probability that is the cargo being carried by the larger vessels covered with matting in the upper part of the print. They are making their way along the Shinkawa canal towards the Nakagawa.

The waterways were also used for passenger transportation. This area, for example, was plied by vessels of the gyotoku-bune, a line providing a regular connection from Gyotoku and Koamicho to the centre of the city.

In Hiroshige's print two such boats are placed in the foreground. They are moving in opposite directions past the Nakagawa *gobansho* or guardpost, which was established in the very first years of Tokugawa rule to keep a check on the import of arms into the city and the export of women. The buildings of the post and two guards can be seen on the bank at the lower left.

The quarters located on both banks of the Shingawa were especially noted for one thing: the businesses reputed to produce the best sake were located here. They flourished through until the early twentieth century.

In this work Hiroshige has not set himself to depicting any sort of sights or even "typical features" of Nakagawaguchi. Here he precisely and convincingly presents something else – the special life of the river, its quiet, self-absorbed atmosphere. This kind of understanding of landscape was characteristic of the artist's finest works from the 1830s and 1840s.

70. The Mouth of the Nakagawa River

Nakagawaguchi (2/1857)

Edo was an unusual city. As early as the middle of the eighteenth century it had 1.3 million inhabitants, making it the largest metropolis in the world.

For comparison: in 1801 London had the population of only 850,000. It should be said, though, that having reached the million mark, Edo's population virtually ceased to grow as it was deliberately controlled. In some areas (mainly in the "lower city") the population density was as high as 178,000 per square mile. But the "urban sprawl" was heavily punctuated by green zones: the gardens of temples and shrines (which numbered some 60,000 in Edo) lay undisturbed alongside heavily built-up districts.

The ties with the natural world were most easily felt outside the central part of the lower city. Here urban development alternated with extensive rice paddies and orchards, while the rivers were quite heavily fished. Fish was one of the staples of the traditional Japanese diet and the main ingredient of delicacies (which quite often amounted simply to a particularly dainty way of serving). The place shown here was noted for its carp – a rare and expensive fish in the Edo period. The fishermen are working within the city, although it is difficult to pinpoint the location. The expression *bara-bara matsu* was probably simply a description of the spaced-out pine trees with eccentrically twisted branches which Hiroshige places across the water from us.

Here, as in many other works in the series, Hiroshige deviated from the depiction of a specific "iconographic" motif, presenting the viewer instead with one more picture of the life of the city – an unexpected one for modern eyes, not used to rural scenes in the context of a great conurbation.

Hiroshige uses the technique of juxtaposed planes to create an effect of "being there". Here it is particularly striking. Through the net being cast in the foreground, we see part of the boat and more of the river.

71. "Scattered Pines"
on the Bank of the Tonegawa River

Tonegawa barabara matsu (8/1856)

The composition here is unusual, with the legs and arms of a boatman acting as "side-flaps" to the scene. Hairy legs so prominently placed evoke distaste among Western scholars of Hiroshige's work and hence a negative reaction to the print that is not found in Japanese literature on the artist. Indignation would seem out of place here.

A characteristic device is being used here: a fragmentary object placed sharply in the foreground and the contrasting juxtaposition of planes. The choice of motif is, however, somewhat unusual, like the horse's rump in No. 86. The unaccustomed view of a very familiar object raises a smile, which in all probability is what the artist intended.

Hiroshige depicts an entirely typical feature of the locality – a ferryman conveying passengers across the Tamagawa (the straw hat of one of them can be seen in the bottom right-hand corner). In the distance we can see a lighthouse marking a sandbar. Behind the trees on the left are the buildings of a shrine dedicated to Benzaiten (a water deity and one of the seven gods of happiness). Such shrines were often placed on spits, which ran far out into the sea or estuary.

This particular shrine was a daughter-house of the temple in Enoshima, Sagami province. It contained a statue of the deity, which according to tradition was the work of Kobo-daishi (774-835), the founder of the Shingon school. The Buddhist "counterpart" of the Benten shrine is the Shingon Kon-juzan monastery. The place depicted was at one time known as Kanamejima ("Fan-Pin Island") because it seemed to hold together the fan-like coastline of this part of Haneda Bay.

72. The Benten Shrine
by the Haneda-no watashi Ferry

Haneda-no watashi Benten-no yashiro (8/1858)

Autumn

The title exactly describes both the content and the atmosphere of the print. *Tanabata-matsuri* – the Festival of the Ox-herd and the Weaver-Girl – is of Chinese origin. It is connected with the ancient legend that the heavenly Weaver-Girl (the star Vega) was separated from her Ox-herd lover (the star Altair), but once a year she is able to meet him by crossing a bridge made by myriads of birds across the Heavenly River (the Milky Way).

Tanabata-matsuri was first observed in Japan in the Nara period (646-794), when all aspects of Chinese culture penetrated onto Japan with particular intensity. The first time it was celebrated at court was in 755, under Empress Koken-Tenno (716-770), on the 7th day of the Seventh Month and that became the established date. By the Edo period the Chinese star cult had become one of the five seasonal festivals (*gosekku*). According to the old Japanese calendar Tanabata-matsuri signalled the onset of autumn, although it fell at the warmest time of the year.

In the sixteenth and seventeenth centuries townspeople and samurai began decorating their homes and private gardens, but it was not until the 1850s that decorations appeared in the streets. Bamboo poles were erected on the roofs of houses with various articles that had a propitiary significance attached to them.

In rural areas prayers were said during the festival for a rich harvest, in the cities for success in one's affairs. With time, the tone of the festival was set more and more by children who were learning calligraphy. Their prayers for success in mastering the skill were accompanied by a particular ritual: to the branches of bamboo they tied *tanzaku*, narrow strips of paper inscribed with verses devoted to the love between the Ox-herd and the Weaver-Girl. As the custom became established, *tanzaku* were written on coloured paper.

Various other symbols of prosperity, wealth and success, cut out of paper, were also attached to the bamboo poles. As can be seen from the print, they included a piece of watermelon, a gourd-shaped bottle as used for sake, wine bowls, fishing nets, fish, *hozuki* fruit (Chinese lanterns), a merchant's abacus. Beneath the abacus in the left part of the print is an accounts book inscribed *daifukucho* ("the book of great happiness"). Another pole deeper in the composition bears a money-box inscribed *kinsen-ryo* – "a thousand gold ryo", an expression meaning a fabulous sum of money.

This work creates a general image of a city festival without any "defining feature", yet it is nonetheless a depiction of a specific place. To the right of Mount Fuji, which is placed precisely on the centre line of the composition, we can see the buildings of Edo Castle, and a little lower the fire-watchtower in the Yaesu quarter where Hiroshige was born and lived to the age of thirty-three. Further down are the warehouses of the Minami Demmacho quarter alongside which the artist's house stood. Henry D. Smith II has suggested that this was the view from Hiroshige's own window.

Part of the house is also shown: in the lower right-hand part there is a corner of the veranda where a light summer kimono (*yukata*) is drying on a special stand, perhaps for the artist himself.

73. The City Decorated for the Tanabata Festival

Shityu han'ei Tanabata-matsuri (7/1857)

The procession in the foreground is a *toryo-okuri* - a ritual observed during the building of a new house. After the ridge-piece had been set up, the carpenters performed a ceremony, which involved prayers and a banquet. The event ended with a procession in which the carpenters and owners of the new building saw the senior craftsman on his way. This is the moment Hiroshige depicted.

The procession is headed by the chief craftsman, carrying a ritual pole decorated with five-coloured ribbons and topped with a *gohei* made of three fans arranged in a circle. The red patch in the centre of each fan is the rising sun, which had a propitiatory significance. The fans are surrounded by a mirror and, below it, hairdressing accoutrements: a comb, two bags of ribbons and a chignon. These elements have a very ancient origin. At one time it was customary to sacrifice a young maiden at the foundation of a building and the articles of female toiletry were a symbolic reminder of this practice.

The chief craftsman is wearing a formal costume decorated with his personal badge. The right to use such a badge was occasionally granted to the inhabitants of the city - the richest and most worthy, of course. On his head is a ceremonial hat (*eboshi*) worn only on ceremonial occasions.

Behind him come the owners of the building, dressed in clothing reminiscent of that worn by the samurai class. They are carrying two *hamaya*, huge ceremonial arrows used in exorcism rituals to drive off evil spirits. The first takes the form of a signal arrow (*kaburaya*) that was fitted with a whistle shaped like a turnip (*kabura*), hence the name. Such arrows were usually used to announce the start of a battle. The second is a hunting arrow with a double tip (*karimataya*). The *kaburaya* was associated with the "male", positive cosmic principle, the yang; the *karimataya* with the "female", negative ying.

Both arrows are decorated with massive relief depictions of a crane among the clouds and a turtle among the waves. Both images are symbolic wishes for longevity with origins in Taoism, one of the main religions of China.

The procession is moving along one of the streets in Odemmacho, a wealthy central quarter of the capital, adjoining the Nihonbashi. This quarter, which appeared as the focus of the transport system linking Edo with the rest of the country, became with time one of the busiest shopping areas in the city. Silk fabrics were the main goods sold here and shops selling them could make up whole streets. The print shows the quarter's Third Street, where the largest firms had their trading premises. The most prominent of such business was Daimaru and the decoration of the awnings and the advertising sign in front of the entrance here feature its trademark - a circle (*maru*) containing the character meaning "big" (*dai*).

The sign proclaims "All sorts of fabric" and, higher up, either side of the trade mark "Payment in cash. Prices are not negotiable." This way of trading was introduced by another cloth dealer in the late seventeenth century (see No. 8).

In the early twentieth century, the fabric shops in Odemmacho became a sight not only for the Japanese, but also for Western tourists. Anna Hartsborn, for example, who visited the country in 1904 had the following to say about the central part of Tokyo: "Then there are the great silk shops, like Dai Maru Ichi and Ichigaya - these also are in Nihonbashi, the busiest part of Tokyo. Far down the street you can hear the din of these big shops, as soon as a customer lifts the curtain, the whole force of clerks and errand boys shout in chorus 'Irashai! - Please come in!'"

This print is among the small number of pure urban landscapes in the series. The theme here is the city, its life and events, not necessarily extraordinary ones.

74. Fabric Shops in Odemmacho

Odemmachô gofukuten (7/1858)

Kanda was situated almost in the centre of what is now Chiyoda, the business sector of Tokyo. At the beginning of the Edo period it was a rice-growing area, which possibly accounts for a name meaning "the Fields of the Gods". It was a custom to send the "first ears" of the new harvest as an expression of gratitude to the Ise shrine, the chief Shinto centre in the country. After the planning of the new capital was complete, Kanda became a craftsmen's district, settled by practitioners of a wide range of trades. There were quarters of blacksmiths, tinsmiths, lacquerers, and so on. The dyers' quarter, Konyacho, lay next door to the blacksmiths' quarter and was inhabited by craftsmen who used an indigo dye to pattern cloth.

Kanda was a special place in Edo. It was the cradle of the capital's urban culture, the culture of the *Edokko* who had their own, highly individual view of the world, a system of values and so on that differed in many ways from those officially propagated. It was considered an honour to belong to the *Edokko*, one which was not easily had. Above all, you had to be at least a third-generation inhabitant of the capital, and to come into the world in one of a limited number of districts, which included Kanda.

There was even a saying: "I am an *Edokko*, I was born in Kanda." It is no coincidence that many artists, particularly *ukiyo-e* painters, came from here.

Hiroshige's print shows us the work of the dyers of Konyacho. Long strips of cloth with patterns in shades of blue, hanging from a wooden frame to dry, occupy the whole of the foreground. These fabrics were intended for light summer kimonos (*yukata*) and towels (*tenugui*) that were also used as headbands to keep perspiration out of the eyes in hot weather.

The designs on the cloth are informative, as they include information about the creators of the series. Two strips of white carry the character for "fish", the first in the name of Uoya Eikichi, the publisher. Another two carry Hiroshige's diamond-shaped seal, made up of two symbols of the Japanese syllabary found in the artist's name: *ro* makes up the frame of the diamond, while *hi* can be read inside it. This is just one of many instances of advertising (and self-advertising) to be found in the details of the pictures – a very common feature of late prints and not always directly connected with the subject of the work.

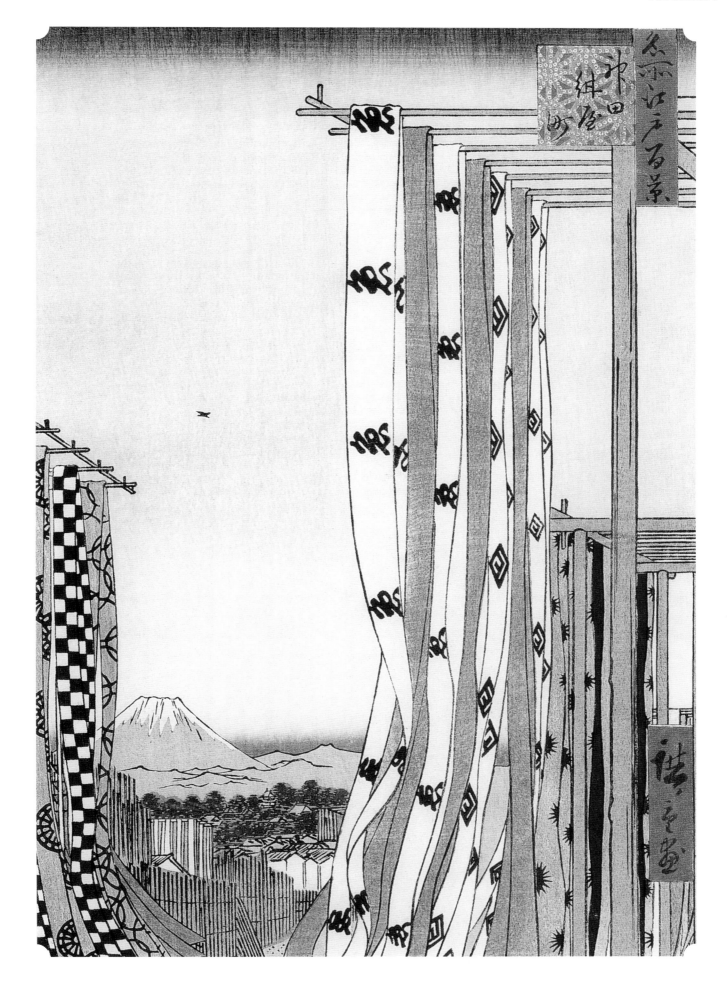

75. The Dyers' Quarter in Kanda

Kanda Kon'yachô (11/1857)

Kyobashi (literally "the Capital Bridge") stands in the centre of Edo – Tokyo. Yet, like many other sights, it relates to the Tokaido highway. Kyobashi was the first bridge on the traveller's way.

After Ieyasu began to organize the new capital, the area around was settled by representatives of various trades. In this way quarters of dyers, blacksmiths and so on appeared. The quarter immediately adjoining the Kyobashi became known in the Kambun era (1661-1673) as Sumicho, the "Colliers' Quarter", on account of the coal-merchants' stores built along the river. No less important for the local economy, however, were the businesses that in one way or another traded in bamboo. Great stocked-up stems of bamboo occupy the whole of the left-hand part of Hiroshige's print. There were also shops here that sold articles made of bamboo and workshops that produced them. The boat on the river is loaded with baskets, boxes and other items woven from bamboo.

In Japan the demand for bamboo was permanently high. Every year, for example, a large number of pieces of bamboo stem were required to create the *kadomatsu*, the main New Year decoration.

The gigantic grass was in even more demand at the Tanabata festival on the 7th day of the Seventh Month (see No. 73), especially after it became fashionable to make a display on the roofs of the houses.

One feature of the Kyobashi bridge is particularly interesting – the onion-shaped finial on the central posts. This *giboshi* (literally "false pearl") marked out the country's most important bridges. In Edo there were only two: the Kyobashi and the Nihonbashi (see No. 1).

A procession of pilgrims are crossing the bridge carrying long bamboo poles with bundles of *gohei*. They are returning from a ritual ascent of Mount Oyama (see No. 60). Another man crossing the bridge has a lantern in his hand that is inscribed with the character *Hori Take*. This literally means "cut out" and "bamboo", but is also a short form of the name Yokogawa Horitake, one of the best *ukiyo-e* woodblock cutters of the mid-nineteenth century. Yokogawa worked on many of Hiroshige's projects and his stamp is commonly found on prints of the period. Two more bridges can be seen in the distance: Nakabashi and Sirauobashi.

76. The Bamboo Bank by the Kyobashi Bridge

Kyobashi takegashi (12/1857)

We look between the masts of two large freight vessels at a canal crossed by a bridge and flanked by buildings of a single type. This is the Hatchobori or "Eight-*cho* Canal" which runs through the central part of old Edo and at its eastern end joins the Sumidagawa not far from Edo Bay. Its name became attached to a quarter between the Kyobashi and Nihonbashi bridges.

The canal was cut in the Kanyei era (1624-1644) and named on account of its length: eight *cho* was about 950 yards. This and other canals were needed because Edo Bay was too shallow to allow large sea-going vessels to come in and moor at piers. Instead they discharged at anchor into small boats that delivered the goods to little jetties by the warehouses. The buildings with white-plastered walls seen here are some of the city's warehouses.

At one time a large number of Shinto shrines and Buddhist monasteries were situated in the Hatchobori quarter, but in the second half of the seventeenth century they were moved to other parts of Edo, chiefly Asakusa. The locality was then occupied by administrative officials (*yoriki* and *doshin*), whom the ordinary people, probably with a touch of humour, called *hatchobori-no danna* –

"the masters from the Eight-*cho* Canal". The *yoriki* were officers of the municipal council. They were all samurai, but not of very high rank and accordingly not highly paid. They made up for this by accepting "voluntary contributions" and became notorious as extortioners. The actual maintenance of law and order on the streets was the responsibility of their assistants, the *doshin*. They were samurai of the lowest rank, permitted to wear only one sword, who commanded a large army of "policemen" recruited from among the ordinary citizens.

The mansions of the *yoriki* and *doshin* can be seen beyond the shrine, half-hidden by the red fence on the left. Minato ("Port") Inari-jinja was one of the oldest Shinto shrines in the Eastern Capital.

In Hiroshige's time it stood at the end of a long sandbar, known as Teppozu – the "Cannon Bar". The name is supposed to have originated when it was used as a testing-range for artillery pieces in the early seventeenth century.

There was a *fuji-zuka* in the precincts of the shrine. It cannot be seen in the print, but the real mountain rises impressively above the grove encircling Inari-jinja.

77. The Minato-jinja Shrine and Inaribashi Bridge at Teppozu

Teppozu Inaribashi Minato-jinja (2/1857)

South of the spot depicted in the preceeding print lay the Akashicho quarter located on the southern tip of Teppozu. When the series was created, Akashicho was a quiet, unremarkable locality. It was customary to rent houses here and install courtesans redeemed from the "green quarters" in them. Only in the 1870s did Akashicho acquire a distinctive "face" as Europeans began to settle here.

The locals made their living by fishing and one of their boats can be seen in the middle distance casting a characteristic rectangular net.

Teppozu – "Firearm Bar" – was long and thin with a shape like the barrel of a gun, hence the name. It formed part of Tsukiji, an area of reclaimed land created in 1658. In the Edo period it contained the mansions of the military elite and monasteries, the most notable of which was Nishi-Honganji. Its tall roof dominates the whole composition of the print.

The monastery was a daughter-house of the celebrated Nishi-Honganji in Kyoto, the chief place of worship for the Jodo Shinshu (Pure Earth) school, one of the varieties of the cult of the Buddha Amida. The monastery in Edo was founded in 1620 by a monk named Junkyo (1577-1630) and moved to this site after the fire of 1657. The main building was completed in 1658. The fishermen resettled by the shogun on neighbouring Tsukudajima (see Nos. 4, 55),

who were followers of Jodo Shinshu, took an active part in the construction work. In 1680 they first performed in the temple a ritual dance devoted to the Buddha Amida and since then it is performed every year at the Bon (Remembrance of the Dead) festival. In the title the temple is called *monzeki* – "a bulwark of faith". This is a special honorific title given to large monasteries of the Jodo Shinshu school.

In *A Hundred Famous Views of Edo* Hiroshige depicted Nishi-Honganji several times (see Nos. 2, 21, 80), but always from a distance. There was a good reason for this: the main building was destroyed by a storm in 1854, and only restored in 1860. When the series was in production, the temple was being repaired and so Hiroshige avoided showing it close-up.

Here and on the following print there is a different title from usual: *Edo hyakkei yokyo* – "Interesting supplements to the prints *A Hundred Views of Edo*". The change was most probably due to the fact that by the time this work appeared (in the Seventh Month of 1858), one hundred prints had already been issued in the series and new ones could therefore be described as supplements. In reality by mid 1858, 109 prints had appeared without the new title, but this can be explained by the works taking different amounts of time to receive the approval of the censor's office, by whose stamps they are dated.

78. The Nishi-Honganji Monastery at Tsukiji, Teppozu

Teppozu Tsukiji monzeki (7/1858)

The place depicted here is still recognizable today. It is the area in front of the Daimon or Great Gate of the Zojoji monastery, approached by a humpbacked bridge across the Sakuragawa Canal (which joins the Fukagawa nearby).

Zojoji was Japan's largest Buddhist centre in the Tokugawa period (see No. 53). The majority of those who studied there were monks of the Pure Earth school, but lay people, and even foreigners, did attend the lectures. One of them was Bishop Nicholas (Nikolai Kasatkin, 1836-1912), the first Orthodox missionary to the islands who was canonized by the Orthodox Church in 1970.

The Daimon with its curved, two-sloped roof has now been restored. Behind it in the print we see the roof of the Sanmon or "Triple Gate" erected in 1622. Its full name is San Gedatsu Mon – "the Gate of the Threefold Liberation". It has three openings, symbolizing the three stages in the attainment of nirvana: elimination of desires, elimination of attachments and union with emptiness. The roof of the main temple (*hondo*) rises slightly above the Sanmon.

To the right we can see another of the sacred places of the Eastern Capital – the Shinto shrine which was commonly referred to as Shiba Shinmei-no miya, although its proper name was Daijingu – "the Shrine of the Great Deity".

Shinmei-no miya was founded in 1005 and dedicated to the deities of the Ise shrine, the chief Shinto holy place in Japan. As a sign of the link between the two, architectural devices typical of Ise, such as the strongly protruding end rafters, were used here.

In Hiroshige's time, the shrine was quite often the venue for theatrical performances, indeed it is reckoned that "temple spectacles" were first put on here. On festivals *sumo* wrestling contests were also held at Shinmei-no miya.

In all probability it is also the destination for the jolly company which Hiroshige places in the foreground. They may be a group of provincials who have come to see the capital at the time of the "Endless Festival" (*daradara-matsuri*) which lasted for a week in the middle of the Ninth Month. They are followed by an orderly group of Zojoji monks headed for the city to collect alms.

79. The Shinmei Shrine and the Zojoji Monastery in Shiba

Shiba Shinmei Zojōji (7/1858)

The Kanasugibashi was built where the Tokaido highway crosses the mouth of the Furukawa (known locally as the Kanasugigawa) not far from the entrance to the Zojoji monastery in the Shiba district (see No. 79).

Shibaura is the name of a part of that district, the stretch of shore from the mouth of the Furukawa as far as Hama-goten, a palace that at various times belonged to various branches of the Tokugawa family, and in the late nineteenth century was reconstructed in the western manner for the reception of noble guests from abroad.

Shiba was the wider coastal district adjoining the Shinagawa. From the outset its character was shaped by two factors. The first was its natural beauty coupled with the proximity of the Tokaido. The area around the Kanasugibashi was always busy with people drawn to the many teahouses, stalls and so on. The second was that, almost from the start of the Edo period, Shiba was full of Buddhist monasteries. The most significant was Zojoji, which from 1590 was the last resting place of shoguns. Today the graves of six of them are in the monastery grounds.

This immense monastery was a city in itself. It shaped the appearance and set the tone for this part of the Eastern Capital, although the present scene has no direct relation to Zojoji. It shows a group of pilgrims who are followers of a different tendency – Nichirenshu, founded by Nichiren (1222-1282).

The pilgrims carry tall poles, one of which has two rows of red and white towels attached to it and is topped by a pair of ritual ladles (*hishaku*). Each of the towels bears a special badge in the form of a branch in a frame and two characters, *koju*, meaning "association". This is a reference to one of the local groups of followers of a particular Buddhist school that formed the smallest structural link in the religious organization of Japan during the Edo period.

Another pole bears a towel with a more specific indication of the congregation: Edo koju. This pole is crowned with an umbrella-like *manto* with attached towels. On these the inscription Minobu-san appears beneath the association's badge.

Minobu-san is a mountain in Yamanashi Prefecture to the south of Mount Fuji. It was there that Nichiren chose to live out his days and there that he was buried.

The Kuonji monastery founded nearby became a place of pilgrimage for followers of his school, particularly in autumn on the anniversary of his death (the 13th day of the Tenth Month).

In all probability the group depicted here are also performing a pilgrimage on that day, to another shrine, but one no less connected with Nichiren and with his death in particular – the Honmonji monastery.

Shortly before his death, Nichiren left his retreat on Mount Minobu and made for the hot springs at Hitachi. On the way he made a stop at the estate of the government official Ikegami Yasumitsu, where he died about a month later. The temple erected there twenty years on became the core of the Honmonji monastery that was destined to become one of the chief centres of the sect not only in the capital, but in Japan as a whole.

Further proof of the adherence of these particular pilgrims is provided by the large red banner which flutters prominently in the foreground. It carries two texts. The lower one is a well-known sacred formula: *Namu myoho renge kyo* – "O Sutra of the Unsurpassed Law!" The other is a statement characteristic of Nichiren's teaching: "Everything existing under heaven
and between the four seas
Is subject to the Unsurpassed Law."

One more detail links the pilgrims with Honmonji – the sticks and distinctively shaped drums seen among them. These flat, oval drums reminiscent of fans were an attribute of the Nichirenshu school. At Honmonji they accompanied the ritual chanting of formulas.

The procession could be headed for the monastery or back from it, either interpretation is possible and the most likely of all is that Hiroshige has shown two groups going in opposite directions. The artist choses this device to stress the festive bustle reigning on the Kanasugibashi bridge.

There is one more curious feature here. The pole at the lower left has towels with a different inscription. It reads: *Uoei shi* – "the Publisher Uoei". *Uoei* is an abbreviated form of *Uoya Eikichi*, the publisher of *A Hundred Famous Views of Edo*. This is a sort of advertisement for the publisher who was perhaps himself a follower of Nichiren.

80. The Kanasugibashi Bridge and Shibaura

Kanasugibashi Shibaura (7/1857)

It might seem that the objects placed in the foreground in this print are random and unconnected with each other. In fact, here more than the other works of the series they are apt and symbolic, forming a sort of puzzle, a play on words and images. For example, one of the foreground elements is a huge cartwheel. The singling out of this motif is directly connected with the place names in the title: *Ushimachi* means "the Ox Quarter" and the wheel belongs to a cart drawn by oxen, while in the 1850s Takanawa was written with characters meaning "tall wheel".

The minor details are also eloquent: the watermelon rind suggests autumn; the worn straw boots (*waraji*) would be associated with the end of a long journey. This was indeed the end of the road for many. It was the edge of the city and at the Takanawa Gate, alongside which the artist has placed us, the Tokaido highway left the capital. The mile-and-a-half stretch of road beyond the gate was Takanawa. Hiroshige returned to this locality several times in *A Hundred Famous Views of Edo*. He shows it from various sides, but always "mentions" certain characteristic details that include the *odaiba*, fortifications built on government orders in 1853-1854.

They are visible in the distance in this print too. Ushimachi was the popular name for what was officially Kurumacho ("the Carts Quarter"), situated either side of the Takanawa Gate. Its history began in 1634 when oxen were brought from Kyoto for the construction of Zojoji (see No. 79), one of the most ambitious architectural projects in all the Edo period. The ox drivers also worked on other buildings and in 1639 they were granted land at Ushimachi on which to settle.

Vehicles drawn by oxen were a rarity in the Edo period. Their use was allowed only to senior figures in the feudal hierarchy and on construction work in three cities, Kyoto, Edo and Nagoya. An ox team was an unusual sight on the streets of Edo, although there were quite a number of the animals kept at Ushimachi (between 120 and 1,000 at different times). Ox carts probably evoked historical reminiscences in the minds of the inhabitants of Edo: they were associated with the courtly culture of the Heian period, when they were the only form of transport used by the high nobility.

In this print too, a fragment of such a conveyance was intended to give a hint of the refined culture of Japanese classical antiquity.

81. The Ushimachi Quarter in Takanawa

Takanawa Ushimachi (4/1857)

There are a relatively small number of prints among *A Hundred Famous Views of Edo* in which the actual landscape view plays a secondary role. In such works it is hard to pinpoint the specific location. This applies, at least to a certain extent, to the present print which shows not so much Edo Bay, seen in the background, as the main room of a teahouse with screen walls (*shoji*) opened.

Alongside the tall-stemmed lamp we see the remains of a festive meal. A porcelain dish (from the Imari factory, judging by appearances) contains leftover pieces of *sashimi*, fish of various kinds prepared and served in a special way. The dish itself stands on a lacquered tray. Alongside is a vessel for washing dishes with a little *sake* cup floating in it. On the other side of the lamp, there is a half-opened fan and a tray with smoking paraphernalia: a tobacco-pouch and a pipe in a case, a tiny brazier to light the pipe and an ashtray. Down at the bottom of the print, on the veranda, we find a low table with a porcelain vessel on it and, on the floor alongside, two large sake bottles, also made of porcelain. A discarded pair of chopsticks also lies on the floor.

In itself the scene is highly persuasive: the banquet has just finished; the guests have just departed and those who received them have also left the room for the moment. It is not really possible even to say that they have left the room, so strong is the sense of their presence. On the right we can see the edge of a geisha's robe. She has been invited to provide music and is now preparing to leave. Next to her is her *shamisen* and the case in which it will be put. But the sensation of actually "being there" becomes even stronger due to a feature on the left-hand edge of the print: on the screen wall, covered with translucent paper, we can clearly make out the shadow of a woman. Judging by the complicated hairstyle with a large number of decorative pins she is a courtesan. She is preparing for bed and has already discarded some of her clothing – the brown cloak on the floor.

The evening is at an end. It began with the admiration of the full moon, which is the "chief protagonist" of the work, illuminating the view seen through the parted screen walls.

The seascape with boats gliding across the still water of the bay by moonlight is captivating, but it is not easy to say exactly where it is. Possibly this is the part of Edo Bay close to the Takanawa-no mon Gate.

That city gate was the real start of a journey along the Tokaido from Edo to Kyoto. The locality was noted for its teahouses and their willing serving-girls. There was an abundance of such establishments in the Shinagawa district, that, properly speaking, began at the gate and they were only slightly less popular than the "green quarters" of Yoshiwara. It would seem that the teahouse depicted in the print stood somewhere here, on the border between Takanawa and Shinagawa. Some Japanese scholars have gone further and identified the spot as Yatsuyama Hill, which certainly stood in the right general area. Today the hill has almost vanished. Its disappearance was directly connected with one of the most dramatic turns in Japanese history.

In 1853 Commodore Matthew Perry entered Uraga harbour with his squadron of "black ships". He brought a message from the President of the United States demanding that Japan open her ports to international trade. He promised to return for an answer in a year's time (a promise he kept). The appearance of the squadron prompted the government to take emergency measures. It was decided to build eleven island-forts (*daiba*) between Shinagawa and Susaki, of which six now exist. The soil to build them was taken from two nearby hills – Gotenyama and Yatsuyama, which became unrecognizable.

One of these forts must have been visible from the room that Hiroshige depicted. The fact that it is not in the print is evidently no accident.

In his landscapes the artist quite often sacrificed "documentary accuracy" for the sake of artistic effect. This is the case here: the crude, inelegant shape of the daiba (see No. 83) could have destroyed the lyrical harmony of the moonlit scene. As a result, the artist created a sort of generalized image of a teahouse in Shinagawa, a place that held an irresistable attraction for the inhabitants of the Eastern Capital.

82. The Moon Above a Headland

Tsuki-no misaki (8/1857)

In Hiroshige's time the southern district of Shinagawa actually lay outside the city. It was famous for its amusement quarters and as the first staging-post on the Tokaido highway, that linked two regions of the main island in the Japanese archipelago – Kanto (with its centre in Edo) and Kansai, whose capital was Kyoto, the residence of the Emperor.

Along this road, goods were moved, *daimyo* travelled in procession, messengers hurried from the western provinces to the east and back. Travelling the Tokaido became a fashionable thing to do, which was reflected in literature and the fine arts. Some made the journey on official or commercial business, others simply for amusement.

In Japan it was customary when seeing someone off on a journey to go part of the way with them. Shinagawa became the parting point on the Tokaido.

Despite the fact that Shinagawa was only five miles from the Nihonbashi, where the Tokaido actually began, the journey to this first halt took a whole day and ended with a farewell banquet in one of the numerous teahouses. There the guests would be served by *meshimori*, whose accommodating ways were well-known beyond Shinagawa.

A special class among the customers of the teahouses were the Buddhist monks studying in the nearby Zojoji monastery (see No. 79).

They had enough time to get back before evening. This was also a thriving commercial centre. From the Takanawa Gate to Shinagawa the Tokaido ran along the coast. The land between it and the sea was filled with a large number of shops. On the other side of Shinagawa they stretched as far as the Kanagawa on both sides of the road. One suggestion is that the abundance of wares on sale along this stretch of coast gave the place its name: Shinagawa means "River of Goods".

The view here is from the second storey of one of the many amusement establishments. Below us we can see the corner of a similar building with the light-filled room upstairs. This is taken to be the Dozo Sagami, the most celebrated establishment in this area of the Eastern Capital.

Almost at its entrance the Torimibashi crosses the Megurogawa river. Although much altered, the bridge still exists today. It runs out to a man-made sandbar (*susaki*) on which the Shinto shrine Susaki-jinja stands behind a *torii* gate. The shrine was dedicated to Benzaiten, the water goddess whom popular belief also reckoned one of the deities of happiness.

In the distance we can see the sails of fishing boats in the estuary where the Megurogawa enters Edo Bay. Further off, almost on the horizon there are two recently constructed coastal defence installations (*odaiba*).

83. A Sandbar in Susaki

Shinagawa Susaki (4/1856)

Here we find ourselves at Meguro, a place that was famous for its temple dedicated to Fudo-myoo (see Nos. 23, 24). A bluff running along the Megurogawa river provides a view far into the distance across rice paddies between which a traveller is leading a horse to the snow-capped summit of Mount Fuji, which was a fine sight from anywhere in Meguro. The slope depicted in the foreground was known as Chayazaka – "Teahouse Slope", a name connected with the title of the print. The story goes that while hunting in the area one of the shoguns made a stop in a little teahouse where he was served by an elderly couple. After that the establishment began to be called Jijigachaya – "Grandpa's Teahouse". Hiroshige depicted it in the bottom right-hand corner. According to some sources, there was not one but two teahouses on the hill. The other, called Babagachaya – "Grandma's Teahouse" – was on the top.

84. "Grandpa's Teahouse" at Meguro

Meguro Jijigachâya (4/1857)

Akasaka was a district in the northern part of the area adjoining the port. It served as a sort of outpost defending the approaches to the shogun's residence.

In the eighteenth and nineteenth centuries it contained the mansions of *daimyo* – the governors of provinces, among others that of Kii, which gave rise to the name Kinokunizaka, meaning the slope running along the eastern edge of the mansion of the ruler of Kii. The grounds of this estate have survived to this day, but the mansion itself has been lost. Now its site is occupied by a guesthouse belonging to the Ministry of the Imperial Court, a western-style building.

The procession of samurai in the print is advancing alongside the Sotobori, the Outer Moat around the shogun's castle. This long moat was one of the grandest and most devious schemes devised by Tokugawa Ieyasu (1542-1616) who moved the capital to Edo. It began from the Sumidagawa in the Asakusa district and ran in a loop gradually approaching the citadel of the shogun's castle. It was an effective defensive feature, but it called for an unprecedented amount of labour and took years and years to complete. That quite suited Ieyasu, who reckoned to involve all the great lords in the project, depriving them of the time, and even more importantly, the funds to indulge in rebellious activities.

Asano Yoshinaga (1576-1613) showed particular zeal during the construction of the moat, for which he was appointed ruler of Kii.

Akasaka has a rugged terrain, constantly rising and falling. The name itself means "Red Slope", for which there are several explanations. The most likely and generally accepted is that the plant madder (*akane* – literally "red root"), which was used in medicine and to produce a red dye, grew here in abundance. The place accordingly became known as Akaneyama, "Madder Hill", and in common speech Akasaka – "Red Slope".

For all its "landscape" character, this print is brimming over with historical associations. Admittedly, many of them are hinted at, rather than presented directly.

This applies, for example, to Tameike – a man-made pond with the shape of a bottle-gourd about two-thirds of a mile long that appeared as a result of a miscalculation during the making of the External Moat.

One of those responsible for the pond's appearance was Asano Sakyodayu Yoshinaga – a prominent, energetic, but not always successful figure of the time. In the early seventeenth century the Asano family was closely tied to the highest power in the land: Yoshinaga's younger brother married shogun, Ieyasu's daughter and became the master of the castle in Hiroshima. The mansion of the Hiroshima branch of the Asano family is also "invisibly present" in the print. We can see only its garden, directly behind the column of samurai.

On the whole the topography of the area is readable here. In the distance, in the centre of the print, we find the fire-watchtower marking the location of the barracks of the shogun's fire-brigade, south of Tameike. The crowns of the trees above Hiroshige's signature conceal the Sanno Shinto shrine (see No. 52). The left-hand edge cuts off a depiction of Akasaka-mon, the gateway into the shogun's castle on this side.

85. The Kinokunizaka Slope with the Tameike Pond in Akasaka in the Distance

Kinokunizaka Akasaka Tameike enbo (9/1857)

In the same way as Tamagawa was the southern gateway to Edo, Yotsuya was the entrance to the capital from the west. Beyind it lay the road leading to the province of Kai. The gate itself is not shown in the print. It should be close to the grove depicted in the depths of the view, behind which lay the boat-station on the Tamagawa river. This grove was the start of the street in the Naito-Shinjuku quarter that Hiroshige depicted.

Naito-Shinjuku was one of the post-stations on the fringes of the Eastern Capital and was founded by a group of entrepreneurs from Yoshiwara as a staging post for the important Koshukaido highway.

Even more than the hairy legs in No. 72, this composition has dismayed connoisseurs of the woodblock print on account of the "vulgar" motif employed. The viewer is asked, as it were, to squat directly under the tail of the horse whose rump occupies three-quarters of the foreground.

This "insulting" position is made worse by other details. The hooves of the two horses in the foreground are shod in the special "sandals" woven from straw which served instead of iron horseshoes in Japan. This element is very carefully depicted, with an "ethnographical" precision. The horses' legs are so fascinating that one does not immediately notice the feet of the groom, clad in similar sandals and so placed that they appear "on a level" with the horses' and are hard to distinguish from them. This kind of device is like a practical joke.

The most shocking thing for the sensitive viewer, however, are the dark spots of horse manure right under his nose.

Here, of course, as with the boatman's legs we are dealing with Hiroshige's sense of humour. This is a joke, not particularly subtle, but funny in its way and, most importantly, appropriate. The tone wholly accords with the character of the locality depicted.

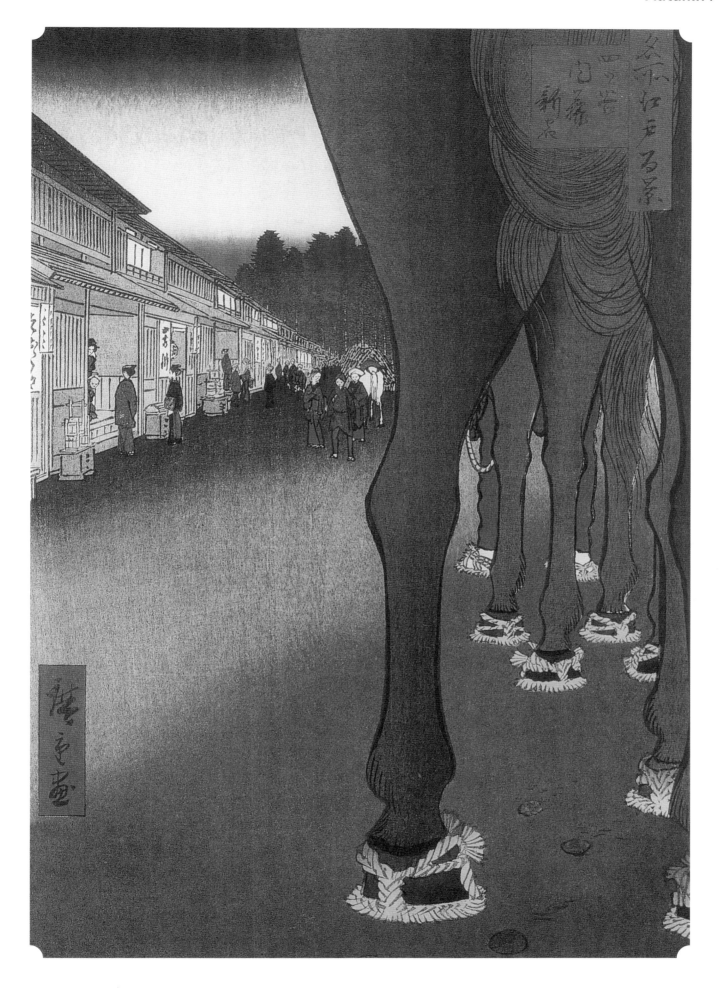

86. Naito-Shinjuku in Yotsuya

Yotsuya Naito-Shinjûku (11/1857)

In no other print in the series does Hiroshige take us so far from the centre as this. Inokashira-no ike is situated in the middle of the Musashi plain, strictly speaking not even in the suburbs. The name of the pond means "Main Source". It appeared relatively late and in all probability was due to the role it began to play in the early seventeenth century.

It entered history about 1590, when Tokugawa Ieyasu came to Edo. Hunting in the surrounding area was more than just an amusement for him. It was a means of reconnoitring for anything that might prove useful to his city.

Once Ieyasu was hunting by this pond and tried the water. He appreciated both its clarity and its taste. The pond was fed by seven underground springs, which gave it its other name – Nanai-no ike, "the Seven Springs Pond". That was a descriptive name, the other was "functional".

In the early seventeenth century, work began on the Kanda-josui aqueduct leading from this pond which never dried out even in the worst drought. For many years this aqueduct was the Eastern Capital's only source of drinking water and it remained an important source right up to the Meiji period. The pond was narrow, but extended for about two-thirds of a mile from north-west to south-east.

In Hiroshige's print we have a view across the pond to the distant Nikko chain including Nantaisan on the left, a celebrated peak that was poetically termed the Fuji of Nikko.

The pond and the mountains are depicted from different points of view: the former from the north-east, the latter from the south. There could be various explanations for this, but one thing is clear: depicting the mountains, especially Nantaisan, with their most familiar outlines, helped to orientate the viewer. Everyone knew that the Nikko chain should be visible from Inokashira-no and everyone knew the characteristic silhouette of Nantaisan that made the place instantly identifiable.

This approach to depicting a locality was not invented by Hiroshige: it occurs quite often in the illustrations to topographical guidebooks of Edo, in which more attention was paid to the relative locations of the features than to precise verisimilitude. The artist also saw the Benten shrine from the south. It is shown in a strictly frontal elevation – the only occasion in the whole series when Hiroshige used such a method of depicting a building. Benten-no yashiro, like almost all shrines to this deity stood in a grove on a small island linked to the mainland by a bridge.

87. The Benten Shrine on Inokashira-no ike Pond

Inokashira-no ike Benten-no yashiro (4/1856)

Takinogawa means "the River of Waterfalls" and one might well think that it is the name of the river shown in the print. In actual fact we are looking here at a section of the Shakujiigawa that runs through the Oji district. Throughout the Edo period this was a rural area, some five miles distant from the city centre, that grew vegetables for sale on the capital's markets.

There was a large number of waterfalls in this area (see No. 49) and one of them is shown on the right-hand edge of the print. This is Benten-no taki, the "Benten Waterfall". Alongside is a lean-to structure put up for pilgrims who come here to perform ritual ablutions.

Further up there is a grotto also dedicated to Benten (Iwaya Benten), the entrance to which is marked by a red *torii* gate. The grotto belonged to a Shinto shrine called Matsubashi Benten, the yellow roofs of which are just peeping from behind the hill.

Further still we find the Matsuhashi ("Pine Bridge") spanning the Shakujiigawa and so linking the Nakasendo highway, leading to Kyoto by way of Shinano, Kazusa and Omi provinces, with the celebrated Oji-gongen shrine. The little road running upwards past the teahouses on the left bank of the river leads directly to the shrine and the associated Kinrinji monastery.

For the inhabitants of Edo the most remarkable place in this locality was one that is barely indicated in the print – Kongoji, a monastery of the Shingon school. The roof of its main temple can just be seen by the right margin of the print, immediately behind the cartouche containing the title of the series. Kongoji was the official name of the monastery.

Popularly, it was known as Momijidera – "the Monastery of the Scarlet Maple Leaves". Viewing maple leaves in autumn was one of the inhabitants traditional seasonal entertainments. The monastery and adjoining area were famous for these trees. They are shown in Hiroshige's print, but due to the decomposition of the pigment used for the foliage, it has become badly blackened.

88. Takinogawa in Oji

Oji Takinogawa (4/1856)

Hiroshige takes us back to the monastery at Ueno (see No. 11) and right up to the tree that the *Edokko* called Tsuki-no matsu – "the Moon Pine".

The meaning of the name is obvious. One of the branches of the tree was bizarrely twisted so as to form an almost perfect circle reminiscent of the full moon. It became the fashion to view that heavenly body through this natural "frame".

In Hiroshige's print, the view through the Moon Pine is of Shinobazu-no ike, the "Impatient Pond". There are two areas of buildings beyond the tree. The nearer one is on the island of Nakajima, which was artificially created almost in the middle of the pond. It is a shrine for the worship of Benzaiten.

The inhabitants of the Eastern Capital liked to visit the Benten (a shortened form of the word) shrine, especially in the first few days of the New Year, when it was customary to make a pilgrimage to temples of the gods of happiness. Ueno (today a city park) had shrines to all seven of these deities on its territory. The pilgrimage began with a visit to the temple on the island.

As is often the case in this series, the most important element of the "sight" is not the focal point of the composition. Here the artist makes the Moon Pine his "chief protagonist", giving it the whole of the foreground. The real "attraction" of the locality, the Benten shrine, is only indicated: its buildings, easily recognizable by the red colour common to all Shinto structures, are shifted to the very edge of the picture and cut off by the margin.

The opposite shore of the pond (Hongodai) was occupied in Hiroshige's time by the mansions of *daimyo*. The mansion marked out by the pine branch is Kagayashiki. In 1616-1617 it belonged to the Maeda clan who ruled the province of Kaga.

The dull, single-coloured buildings of the mansion form the background for the landscape as a whole, but the dominant element here is the fire-watchtower.

89. The "Moon Pine" in the Precincts of the Monastery at Ueno

Ueno sannai Tsuki-no matsu (8/1857)

In this series Hiroshige devotes much attention to the "green quarters" of Yoshiwara and to the routes by which they are reached. This was quite natural. Yoshiwara was a focal point of the distinctive urban culture, a centre with a tremendous attraction for all the inhabitants of the Eastern Capital and for visitors. The only attraction that could rival it was the *Kabuki* theatre, a new form of performing art that appeared and developed in the Edo period. As with all other aspects of life, the Tokugawa government strictly regulated everything connected with the theatre. Only three companies were permitted in the Eastern Capital and their theatres were all in a special quarter in the Ginza district. In 1841, however, a fire reduced those buildings to ashes. Subsequently, the capital's three main theatres – Nakamuraza, Ichimuraza and Moritaza – were moved to the outskirts, to the Asakusa district, which was by then the location of the "green quarters" of Yoshiwara.

The theatres were relocated to the former suburban residence called Koide Shinano-no mori and the area was renamed Saruwakamachi after Saruwaka Kanzaburo who came to Edo in 1624 and founded the first theatre in the city (Nakamuraza). He is reckoned to be the founder of *Kabuki* in the Eastern Capital.

The theatres stood in a row on the right-hand (western) side of Saruwaka-machi. Each of the buildings had a special superstructure (*yagura*) indicating that it was a licensed theatre. In this print they appear in order of seniority: the first, furthest from the viewer and closest to the gate of the quarter, was Nakamuraza, then came Ichimuraza, and in the foreground Moritaza, as is verified by the inscription on the stack of fire-buckets in front of the entrance.

All the theatres are closed and the street is almost deserted in comparison with the usual crush and bustle. The reason is the time of day: performances began fairly early in the morning and went on all day; by evening, though, a relative calm descended on Saruwakamachi. Only the teahouses shown on the left of the print remained open. There may, however, be another reason for the theatres being closed: the full moon could be an indication that we are in the middle of the Eighth Month, the start of the annual closed season which lasted until the 9th day of the Ninth Month.

The print shows visitors departing from Saruwakamachi: servants from the teahouses light the way for customers. Some will take palanquins, one of which stands ready in the centre.

90. The Saruwakamachi Quarter by Night

Saruwakamachi yoru-no kei (9/1856)

The scarlet leaves of the maple are a sign of autumn in many parts of the world, but in Japan much attention was devoted to the changing colours of foliage. It became a profound aesthetic experience, the theme of poetry and painting. Naturally maples featured in the "autumnal" section of Hiroshige's series, but only in this print has the colour effect that the artist intended survived down to the present day. Different red pigments were used here that did not decompose and darken to the point of complete blackness as in two other autumnal prints in the series (see Nos. 88, 94).

These are the grounds of the Akiba-daigongensha shrine, situated at Ukeji, a village in the Mukojima district, some three miles from the city centre.

From early times this had been a place for the worship of Inari, the harvest deity who is often depicted with, or in the guise of, a vixen. Around 1700 the cult of Inari merged with that of another Shinto deity – the fire god Akiba-daigongen whose chief shrine was in Totomi province close to the Tokaido highway. Travellers often called in there, which increased its popularity. In 1702 the main building (*shinden*) of the shrine at Ukeji was erected on the funds of Prince Honda.

The shrine was dedicated to a deity that gave protection against fire. It was particularly venerated by the women of high-placed families, including the shogun's, and so enjoyed important support.

A statue of the chief deity was set up in the *shinden*. It took the form of a *tengu* – a mythological monster, in this instance with human form. The *tengu* stood, holding a sword in its right hand and a cord in its left, on the back of a white fox, against a background of tongues of flame. In the gardens to the west of the Shinden lay the pond that Hiroshige depicted. The same work remarks that the scarlet leaves of the maples are especially attractive here reflected in the quiet water of the pond. This too is recorded by Hiroshige who most probably saw everything and set it down on paper. At the lower left, on the veranda of the tea pavilion that stood on the bank of the pond, we see a shaven-headed monk sat sketching. There is a very probable theory that this figure is Hiroshige himself. The artist became a monk in the Third Month of 1856, just over a year before this print was published, and his habit of sketching from life is well known – quite a number of his sketchbooks have survived.

91. In the Precincts of the Akiba Shrine at Ukeji

Ukeji Akiba-no keidai (8/1857)

Hardly anything of what is "promised" in the title actually appears in the print: we cannot see the monastery and the Gozensaihata area is barely indicated. Another attraction is placed in the foreground. Two women are descending from a boat and making for a large building with a veranda. This is Uehan, a famous restaurant in the nineteenth century, serving dishes of sweet potatoes and shellfish.

The bridge across the Uchigawa visible behind the restaurant leads to an area of which we only see a small fragment on the left-hand side of the print. This was Gozensaihata – a rather strange name meaning "His Excellency's Snack". At one time this spot was used by the shogun for falconry. Then, about the 1650s, they began growing all sorts of vegetables here. The produce was delivered to the shogun's court.

By Hiroshige's time nothing remained of this practice apart from the name and he shows only a small section of riverbank dotted with pines.

The main sight of this area is the Mokuboji monastery, in whose grounds Uehan stood, but its buildings are not shown. The monastery was founded in the Jogan era (976-978). Its name is inseparably associated with the sad story of Umewakamaru, the young son of a courtier, who was kidnapped by a slave trader and taken far away. The boy was not up to such a journey and died on the road of hunger and privations. The local villagers buried him and planted a willow on his grave. A wandering monk built a prayer-house alongside that later developed into the monastery. Mokuboji was, and still remains, a popular place of pilgrimage.

92. The Mokuboji Monastery, the Uchigawa River and the Gozensaihata Fields

Mokuboji Uchigawa Gozensaihata (12/1857)

There were many ferries in Edo, indeed they were perhaps the most important means of transport within the city, and Hiroshige depicted them repeatedly. Only in this print, however, does the artist show us a ferry landing, the place where crossings start and finish.

This is the landing of the Niijuku ferry that crossed the Nakagawa, an arm of the Tonegawa that flowed into Edo Bay. Its course was to the north of the Senju-bashi bridge (see No. 103), joining two settlements, Kameari on this bank and Niijuku, which is indicated here only by two buildings with yellow roofs, across the river.

In the print one ferry-boat is moored, while the other is just casting off. The broad steps down to the water are flanked by the buildings of two restaurants that were quite well-known in Edo: the two-storey Chibataya on the left and Fujimiya (of which only the roof is visible) on the right.

As is the case with other "parting places" (the city centre is about seven and a half miles away here), Hiroshige places the viewer looking away from the city, as if intending to leave the capital.

93. The Niijuku-no watashi Ferry

Niijûku-no watashi (2/1857)

We have a view here into the distance across the flat country around Mama with its buildings, ponds and groves.

The diverse, skilfully constructed landscape is shown from between the forking branches of a large maple, whose scarlet leaves hang down right in front of the viewer's eyes. This remarkable tree was for a long time the main sight of the whole area. This immense maple – two men could not embrace its trunk – grew in the precincts of Guhoji, a monastery with an ancient history. The grounds of the monastery had a reputation as a fine place to admire the autumnal foliage, mainly due to this one tree. The monastery buildings cannot be seen: they are behind our back and the artist directs our gaze to the Shinto shrine called in his day Tekona-no yashiro.

This shrine, and the entire locality, are associated with a story related in Manyoshu, the earliest anthology of Japanese poetry (mid eighth century).

Tekona, a village girl from Mama, became so famous for her beauty that she was courted by high-ranking suitors from all over Japan. The sensitive girl was driven to despair because she was the cause of discord between such worthy men and she drowned herself in a river near her home. Her grave survived down the years and in the sixteenth century a shrine named after her formed around it.

Manyoshu also mentions the Tsugihashi, a small bridge painted red. Its name means "Linking Bridge" and may come from the fact that it connected two other bridges. Mountains rise behind the shrine and groves. The distinctive silhouette of twin-peaked Tsukuba identifies the Nikko range, but they cannot be seen from this angle from Guhoji. Henry D. Smith II has suggested that Tsukuba appears here as a literary allusion: in Manyoshu verses dedicated to Tekona follow straight after the songs about Tsukuba.

94. Scarlet Maple Trees at Mama by the Tekona-no yashiro Shrine and the Tsugihashi Bridge

Mama-no momiji Tekona-no yachting Tsugihashi (1/1857)

Konodai is still one of the best places from which to view Mount Fuji. This hill dropping precipitously to the Tonegawa river is strongly associated with Japan's warlike past.

It is supposed to have got its name during the campaign of Jimmu-tenno (seventh century B.C.), the semi-legendary first ruler of Japan, to the eastern regions. A swan was spotted on this eminence and it accordingly became Konodai – "Swan Hill".

The hill was very valuable from a military point of view since whoever held it could control an extensive area. Consequently the top of the hill was fortified.

After the Ashikaga clan won a power-struggle in the first part of the fourteenth century, Kyoto again became the capital and the eastern regions which gravitated towards Kamakura – the earlier capital, situated not far from Edo – became of secondary importance for a time. This state of affairs lasted until a third force, the Hojo clan, appeared in the east. A war began for domination of the area and the Hojo gained one victory after another.

At that time Konodai and its castle, Ichikawa-jo, belonged to the Satomi clan, opponents of the Hojo. The fate of this clan proved tragic.

In 1538 the united forces of Asikaga and Satomi were crushingly defeated by the Hojo army and Ichikawa-jo was lost. The Satomi managed to preserve their army, but were forced to avoid major clashes for a time and recover their strength.

The decisive battle for the hill took place in 1564. Yoshihiro, then head of the Satomi clan, defeated the forces of Hojo Ujiyasu and recovered the castle. Once inside his warriors began celebrating heavily and continued all night. By morning they were in no state to fight and Hojo Ujiyasu's men easily beat them. Of the 8,000 Satomi warriors who had fought for the castle the day before, 5,000 died in this second battle. The clan survived, but never again involved itself in military affairs.

The Ichikawa-jo castle was torn down on the orders of Tokugawa Ieyasu at the very end of the sixteenth century. In the Edo period the hill itself changed shape due to a landslide, leaving a cliff-like slope above the Tonegawa. This was the best spot for viewing Mount Fuji as three figures are doing in the print.

Heavily laden freight vessels are sailing along the river towards the south. They are making for the centre of the capital which they will reach by way of the Shinkawa and Onagigawa canals.

95. View of Konodai Hill and the Tonegawa River

Konodai Tonegawa fukei (5/1856)

These two villages were on the outskirts of the Eastern Capital, in an area alongside the left bank of the Edogawa river. The existence of the river is indicated here only by the masts of two boats seen in the depths of the print below and to the right of Mount Fuji. Two groups of buildings are shown in the centre, on either side of the Sakaigawa canal. Nekozane on the right and Horie on the left are linked by the Sakaibashi bridge. We are looking at them from the direction of Edo Bay.

These two villages were noted for the fact that they supplied the city markets with a particular edible shellfish (*bakagai*).

These molluscs were gathered on the many sandbanks located where the Edogawa flowed into the sea. The name *bakagai* is rather strange, one of the ways in which it was written means "stupid shell". As well as fishing and gathering shellfish, the local inhabitants also occasionally hunted birds. In the foreground we can see one of the methods that they used. The birds here are grey sandpipers (*daizen*).

A net was buried just under the surface of the sandy shore and the area sprinkled with bait. When enough birds had gathered, the men tugged on a long rope attached to the net and it closed over them.

96. Horie and Nekozane

Horie Nekozane (2/1856)

Many place names in old Edo were connected with trees and pine-trees in particular, probably because they were perceived as symbols of longevity. Among such place names is Gohonmatsu, which literally means "Five Pines". At one time there were indeed five trees here, but by the early nineteenth century four had been lost. The remaining tree, which grew in the grounds of the Kuki mansion, survived until the end of the century. The unusual shape of the old pine attracted people's attention and became a local sight. It was customary to observe the moon from here, and a poem was even composed on this score:

Ten people
Gathered to admire the full moon
And all by the one pine.

The Kuki estate adjoined the Onagigawa canal that linked the Sumidagawa and Nakagawa rivers (see No. 70). The mansion lay roughly halfway between the Mannenbashi (see No. 56) and the point where the canal joined the Nakagawa. The Jukkengawa canal ran parallel to the Onagigawa and was connected to it by a small channel close to Gohonmatsu. The small humpback bridge visible through the branches of the pine marks the end of this channel.

In Hiroshige's print the canal bends fairly sharply to the right. In reality, though, the Onagigawa was as straight as an arrow. Here the artist clearly and deliberately deviates from topographic accuracy. The invented curve made it possible to show features – such as the little bridge just mentioned – that would otherwise be out of sight.

97. The "Gohonmatsu Pine" on the Onagigawa Canal

Onagigawa Gohonmatsu (7/1856)

The spectacle we witness here can be taken as a precise, symbolic expression of the essence of Edo's urban culture – the last and most individual manifestation of traditional Japanese culture. This is a night view with the dark sky occupying almost two-thirds of the picture, yet the scene is brightly lit by a glittering display of aerial fireworks.

The Ryogokubashi was a special place in the capital. The bridge itself was built in 1659-1661 to the design of the government officials Shibayama Genyemon and Tsubouchi Tozaemon. It was the second bridge across the Sumidagawa and the second in terms of size, after the Senju-Ohashi. The area by the bridge might be called the "carnival district". All sorts of amusements, celebrations and festivities took place around the bridge – on land and on the water.

The celebrations connected with the "beauties of the season" were widely celebrated here: admiring the cherry blossoms in spring; looking at the snow-covered banks of the Sumidagawa in winter; and in summer letting off fireworks. Most popular of all, though, in the warm part of the year were *funaasobi* – "entertainments afloat".

The district offered a variety of attractions, including teahouses with their own distinctive features and a two-and-half-mile dyke which was a conventional place to stroll.

In the Kyoho era (1716-1736), the eighth shogun, Yoshimune, ordered the dyke planted with cherries, peaches and willows – 150 trees of each kind. The greatest sight associated with the Ryogokubashi was, however, the "flower fires" or *hanabi*.

At first fireworks were imported from China, where they had been invented in the distant past, but in 1659 an entrepreneur named Yabei opened his own factory in Edo. Soon the popularity of fireworks was so great that the government was forced to issue special decrees banning them for fear of fires. By Hiroshige's time, the manufacture, sale and, on the more critical occasions, launching of fireworks was in the hands of two businesses: Kagiya (Yabei's firm) and Tamaya. They always participated in the displays by the Ryogokubashi. The *hanabi* reached their peak when on the orders of Shogun Yoshimune (1684-1751) Kagiya prepared a special display as part of an enormous purification ritual intended to drive off the spirits of famine and epidemic that were then afflicting the country. This event, which took place on the 28th day of the Fifth Month of 1733, became the first Kawabiraki ("Opening of the River"). This ceremony is still held today (although there have been breaks in the tradition).

The occasion was attended by enormous numbers of people. It was a truly popular festival – everybody would be at the Ryogokubashi. The crowd on the bridge was so dense that it was impossible to move, while the boats were so thick on the river below near the bridge that the water could not be seen. Other suitable vantage points were the many establishments situated around the adjacent Yanagibashi bridge (see No. 32). It is the view from the window of one such place that Hiroshige reproduces in this print.

During the fireworks displays boats of many kinds appeared on the river. They included the large excursion vessels known as *yakatabune* – "palace-boats" which were only hired by very wealthy merchants and only for special occasions. This is probably the reason why they are so rare in *A Hundred Famous Views of Edo*.

The example in this print – the larger vessel hung with lanterns this side of the bridge – is the only one in the series. Around it are smaller boats: the roofed *yanebune* and the *chokibune*, "boar's tusk", so-called because their prows pointed sharply upwards. The boat with a single lantern hanging from a pole in the prow that can be seen near the right-hand end of the bridge heading towards the *yakatabune* is an *urourobune*, a sort of floating snack-bar.

The idea of fireworks by the Ryogokubashi was firmly connected with the Kawabiraki (the 28th day of the Fifth Month), but that can hardly have been the occasion depicted here. The fireworks season did indeed start at the end of the Fifth Month but it went on to the very start of autumn, finishing on the 28th day of the Eighth Month, when a final performance was given. This is most probably what was intended here: the additional "contents sheet" to the series that groups the prints by season places this particular work in the "Autumn" section.

98. Fireworks by the Ryogokubashi Bridge

Ryogoku hanabi (8/1858)

Winter

Kinryuzan (literally "the Mountain of the Golden Dragon") was one of the three oldest and most important centres of Buddhism in the Eastern Capital. It was founded in the 36th year of Empress Suiko's reign (627) when the religion was still taking its first steps in Japan. The best period for Sensoji, as the monastery was more often called, began in 1589 when Tokugawa Ieyasu took notice of it. The monastery's standing was further enhanced when the memorial shrine (Toshogu) of the first Tokugawa shogun was constructed here. Although the Toshogu was later moved, Sensoji retained firm ties with the ruling family. Its popularity was also greatly bolstered by the fact that it stood alongside the Eastern Capital's most celebrated pleasure quarters. (The "green quarters" of Yoshiwara were relocated here in 1657). Besides which, in the early 1840s the city's three main *Kabuki* theatres were moved to Saruwakamachi which adjoined the monastery on the north-east.

Sensoji appears several times in the series, but in this print, which opens the "winter section", Hiroshige "enumerates" the main buildings of the complex. In the foreground is the *kaminarimon* or "Thunder Gate". It was built in 1633, burnt down three times, but its most precious feature – statues of the gods of thunder and wind that stood in niches either side – were saved each time and it was always restored. The gate statues played an important role in the monastery's life. They were put up at the grand entrance in order that wind and thunder would come at opportune moments and the gods would protect the monastery.

All the upper part of the gateway is taken up by an enormous paper lantern on which we can see the character *hashi* ("bridge") and above it the symbol for n. This is the end of the word Shinbashi – the area where those who donated the lantern lived. Their names are inscribed on the lacquered wooden base of the lantern between the *manji* (swastikas) – an ancient symbol which was taken up in Buddhist iconography as a representation of charity, appeasement and perfection.

Through the gate we have a view of a five-tier pagoda, one of two that once stood in the monastery. To the left of it is another gate, the Niomon, beyond which stands the *hondo* (main temple) dedicated to the bodhisattva Kannon.

The Niomon was one of the Edo period's finest pieces of architecture. As the name suggests, sculptures of the Nio, the guardians of the monastery, stood there in niches. According to tradition, these statues were created by Unkei, one of the greatest figures in the history of Japanese sculpture. Among ordinary people the statue standing on the right was especially popular. It was of Kongorikishi who was also considered a healer deity, particularly efficacious for children's smallpox. Infants were invariably brought to the gate in an effort to secure his support.

The Kaminarimon and Niomon are linked by a broad path about 270 yards long. This central approach to the monastery was called Nakamise ("the middle or inner shops"). This street or quarter formed around 1700. In Hiroshige's time temporary stalls were put up during trading times and then dismantled. They do not appear in the print, which depicts a snowy winter's day. The few people to be seen have their backs to us and are moving towards the Niomon. They seem to hug the side of the path, leaving the central part empty.

Such a depiction of a busy part of the city was not typical of Hiroshige himself and does not accord with the real state of affairs in this locality. As always, the artist concentrates on depicting the "main character" or "chief motif" of the chosen locality, omitting everything that might disrupt the integrity of the image. Here the main motif is the majestic monastery buildings.

99. The Kinryuzan Monastery in Asakusa

Asakusa Kinryuzan (7/1856)

In the series, the artist thoroughly traces the route leading to the famous "green quarters" of Yoshiwara. The journey was a long one, and the last stretch of it ran alongside the Sanyabori canal.

Here, by the Imadobashi Bridge (see No. 34), the pleasure-seeker disembarked from the small boat that had usually been hired by the Yanagibashi (see No. 32) and continued on foot or in a palanquin.

The embankment, or more precisely dyke, along the canal appeared in the first half of the seventeenth century, following the flood that seriously affected the Asakusa district in 1619.

The dyke also had another name – Dote-hatte, the "Eight-*cho* Embankment" (1 *cho* = 119 yards). In reality it was somewhat longer: the distance from the bridge where the *chokibune* tied up to the main gate of Yoshiwara was roughly 500 yards.

The print shows the last section of the dyke. The journey's end is near. We can already see, on the right, the green crown of the tree that was known as "the Parting-Glance Willow". It stood at the bottom of the slope that led up from the dyke to the main gate of Shin-Yoshiwara. The visitor leaving the "green quarters" in the early morning would turn round here for a last look before heading for home.

100. The Nihonzutsumi Embankment at Yoshiwara

Yoshiwara Nihonzutsumi (4/1857)

In this print we find ourselves upstairs in one of the pleasure houses of Yoshiwara. The room is in a state of slight disorder. A towel decorated with a feather motif is carelessly draped on the windowsill, creating the impression that it has just been used. Next to the towel is a bowl for rinsing the mouth. There is no-one in the room, but the presence of its mistress is clearly sensed. In all probability, she is behind the screen, the edge of which takes up all the left side of the print. This is the back side of the screen, the black silk lining woven with stylized birds.

Other birds form the design on the panelling beneath the window. They are conventional depictions of sparrows which are most often termed *fukura-suzume* – "sparrows of happiness", a common propitiatory symbol. Such birds might, however, also be referred to as *Yoshiwara-suzume* – "Yoshiwara sparrows", the nickname given to regular visitors to these quarters who knew their customs and traditions. The sobriquet was sometimes applied to those who came to Yoshiwara simply to look at its women, in this instance, though it is clearly an allusion to a regular client who has recently left the courtesan now resting behind the screen. There are several indications of this, including the roll of toilet paper – a very mundane article, but one which in prints, especially as a characteristic attribute of courtesans in *bijin-ga*, had a suggestive meaning.

Judging by the lighting, the scene takes place in daytime, which is somewhat unusual. Generally clients could be entertained in Yoshiwara only from late in the evening. This rule was laid aside only on special days when all three entrances to Yoshiwara were opened (two entrances were ordinarily kept closed) and anyone was permitted to enter, even ordinary women of the city.

One of these special days did indeed coincide with the festival of the neighbouring shrine, Washi-no daimyojin. The shrine was the Shinto "partner" of Chokokuji, a Nichiren Buddhist monastery, and effectively stood in its grounds.

At Washi-no daimyojin a deity was venerated in the form of an eagle (*washi* means "eagle") on whose back stood the bodhisattva Myoken, the embodiment of the constellation of the Great Bear and in popular beliefs a bringer of happiness and prosperity.

In the opinion of Henry D. Smith II, the image of the eagle became the basis for a variety of plays on the word *tori* meaning "bird" or (written differently) "chicken". Among other things, one of the festivals of the shrine was called Torinomachi – "the Fair on the Day of the Chicken". This took place once a year, on the 1st Day of the Chicken in the Eleventh Month.

This was effectively the festival of Washi-daimyojin, celebrated in three such shrines dotted around Edo. In the 1770s and 1780s the Torinomachi in Asakusa became the most popular, due in no small part to the proximity of Yoshiwara.

The festival was especially welcomed by the owners of teahouses, restaurants, theatres and "pleasure houses", any business that needed to attract the public. This is reflected in another pun contained in the word Torinomachi: *tori* can also mean "to receive (guests)".

The shrine stood in Asakusa tanbo ("Asakusa Fields"), an area between Okuyama, the commercial and amusement quarter adjoining the Sensoji monastery and Yoshiwara. It was a lonely area of marshes, ponds and flooded rice paddies, just as we see through the window. We are joined in viewing by a white cat sitting on the windowsill. It belongs to a Japanese breed distinguished by the lack of a tail. The shrine itself is not shown in the print, it is off to the left, but that is where the large procession is headed. Many of the participants carry long poles topped with something resembling a broom or rake. These were *kumade* ("bear's claws") a special feature of the Torinomachi festival. They were propitiatory symbols, a sort of amulet intended to bring wealth and success in one's affairs. Representations of a whole variety of objects were attached to these "rakes": a *takarabune* or "ship of treasures" that, apart from precious objects, also conveyed the "seven gods of happiness"; rice-sacks, money-boxes and packets of coins – symbols of prosperity; an arrow embedded in a target – a symbol of wishes fulfilled; a sacred cord (*simenawa*) as protection against misfortunes; a mask of O-Fuku and little figures of Daikoku and Ebisu, gods of happiness who gave an untroubled life; and finally a turtle and a crane, ancient, generally accepted symbols of longevity.

The craftsmen of the nearby quarters made gigantic *kumade* (such as we see in the procession) that were fastened to the ceilings of shops and so on to encourage customers. The main purchasers were "businesses": establishments in Yoshiwara, teahouses, restaurants, places connected with the theatre, boat jetties and the like. Private individuals preferred *kumade* of more modest size, such as Hiroshige places inside the room. These miniature versions take the form of pins for a woman's coiffure. This is a gift for the courtesan, a set of four *kumade*-hairpins in a special paper case, left by the client who has just departed. One pin has been taken out to be examined, and probably praised. In the prints of *A Hundred Famous Views of Edo*, the lack of a human presence is always deceptive.

101. The Torinomachi Pilgrimage
in the Asakusa Rice Paddies

Asakusa tanbo Torinomachi mode (11/1857)

The three villages mentioned were next to Yoshiwara on the one side, and on the other adjoined the Oshukaido, the highway that connected the capital to the northern provinces. They stretched one after another for quite a distance from south to north. Here we are in Minowa, looking at Mikawashima through the territory of Kanasugi.

Although all three villages were incorporated into the capital in 1745, the area remained rural throughout the Edo period. It grew rice and various vegetables, being especially noted for the *daikon*, a large strongly flavoured radish that is an important ingredient in traditional Japanese cookery. Its chief distinction, however, was that the shogun came here to hunt with falcons. The objects of the hunt were the cranes shown in the foreground of the print. They are Japanese red-crested cranes (*tancho*), an endangered species today. From ancient times in China, and then in Japan, the crane was regarded as a symbol of longevity, the companion of the Taoist immortals (*hsian*) and their embodiment. Nevertheless, or perhaps because of this, cranes were hunted and their meat eaten. The shogun's hunt was not a mass slaughter: only one or two birds were taken,

the first by the shogun himself. The trophy was decoratively arranged and dispatched to Kyoto for the emperor's table. This offering was clearly symbolic in nature, expressing wishes for longevity.

The hunt was possible only in winter, when the cranes migrated to Japan from the continent, and in general the birds were protected and fed, which is what Hiroshige has depicted. The inhabitants of Mikawashima constructed little areas enclosed with straw (part of one can be seen by the tree on the far right) where food for the birds was scattered. That is probably what the man seen in the middle distance is carrying. The villagers took turns to guard the feeding areas to make sure the birds were not disturbed by people or dogs. Concern for their welfare went so far that special decrees were issued banning excessive noise or kite-flying in their winter nesting grounds.

It remains to be said that this particular print was "noted" in the West. In Western European and Russian applied art, especially porcelain, there are quite a number of works that draw on elements here, sometimes quite directly, more often in an adapted manner. (The same is true of the figure of an eagle in No. 107.)

102. The Villages of Minowa, Kanasugi and Mikawashima

Minowa Kanasugi Mikawashima (i5/1857)

The Sumidagawa was the main river of the Eastern Capital; the Senju-Ohashi was the first, and largest, bridge over the river. Concerned with domestic stability, the Tokugawa government did not on principle encourage the construction of bridges across major rivers, but the traffic between Edo and the northern provinces of Honshu island was exceptionally intensive and a bridge across the Sumidagawa, connecting the centre of the city with the Oshukaido highway leading northwards was a necessity. It was built in 1594 using the evergreen wood *inumaki*, that is resistant to rot. The Senju-Ohashi was the first bridge across the Sumidagawa and it stood the longest, being destroyed by a flood only in 1885.

The bridge played a significant role in the life of the capital. Roughly a quarter of the *daimyo* coming to Edo for their compulsory annual period of residence entered the city across the Senju-Ohashi, and the shogun himself used it when he travelled to the Nikko mausoleum.

Within a few years quarters sprang up on either side of the bridge, whose functions were determined by the proximity of the highway. This was the location, for example, of one of Edo's four official post stations.

For the inhabitants of Edo this locality also held literary associations. The Senju-Ohashi was the starting point for a celebrated journey around the northern provinces made by the poet Matsuo Basho (1644-1694), which he described in his classic work *Okunohosomichi* ("*Along the Paths of the North*").

As in many prints of the series the vertical composition culminates in a distant mountain – Buko, one of the peaks of the Chichibu-santi chain.

103. The Ohashi Bridge in Senju

Senjû-no Ohashi (2/1856)

Hiroshige's grounds for choosing to depict the village of Koume as one of the hundred sights of Edo are not quite clear. This locality on the east bank of the Sumidagawa was far from lively, perhaps even somewhat cheerless. Yet it does have a certain charm, a special sense of calm and remoteness from the bustle of the central, "commercial" districts of the city.

The village lay in the Honjo district, about two-and-a-half miles from the city centre. At one time it was the location of a mansion belonging to the Mito clan, a side branch of the Tokugawa house. Apart from agriculture, the locals also produced tiles. The name of the place is descriptive: plums (*ume*) grew here in large numbers. Koume and the surrounding area also acquired a certain fame from the Hikifunegawa canal, on the bank of which Hiroshige places us. It was the successor to the aqueduct dug at the start of the Edo period that supplied the Honjo and Fukagawa districts with water. By the beginning of the eighteenth century that water source had become unnecessary and in the 7th year of the Kyoho era (1722) it was abandoned and the course of the aqueduct was taken by the canal used mainly for transport freight.

But its narrowness meant that the barges had to be pulled by men walking along the bank. This practice, unique in Edo, gave its name to the canal – *hikifune* means "tow-boat" – and also to Hikifunegawa, the tow-path running along the embankment. The dyke itself had several names. The section near the village of Koume-mura depicted in the print was known as Koumezutsumi. Such boats can be seen in another print (No. 33), but Hiroshige did not include them here.

Nor did he include the plum trees that gave the place its name. The deciduous trees in the foreground frame the children playing with puppies under them, and in the distance are Japanese alders (*hannoki*) which grew everywhere in this damp, low-lying area.

The view of the canal is almost from its northern end. The banks are linked by bridges – the Hachitanmebashi, Koshinbashi and Shichihonmatsubashi.

A fourth bridge, not visible due to the bend in the canal, led to the Akiba-jinja shrine (see No. 91), the location of which is indicated by the pine-grove on the horizon.

104. The Koume Embankment

Koumezutsumi (2/1857)

Ommayagashi was on the western bank of the Sumidagawa to the north of the government rice-stores. The name and that of the Ommaya-no watashi can be translated as "Stables Embankment" and "Stables Ferry", which exactly describes their location since up until the 1790s the adjoining quarter was occupied by the shogun's stables.

The ferry was in frequent use. It was allocated eight boats, one of which is approaching the bank in the foreground. The passengers are two prostitutes (*yotaka*, literally "night-hawks") and their bodyguard, a *gyu* ("bull-calf").

Yotaka were the lowest kind of prostitute, practising their trade on the street. In the early Edo period they walked around with a straw mat rolled up under their arm in search of clients.

By Hiroshige's time, they took men to woodsheds and temporary stalls which were left empty by traders at night. *Yotaka* had a terrible existence, dealing with the dregs of society and taking shelter in hovels on the canal banks of the Honjo district. They suffered from the diseases typical of their profession and tried to conceal the visible signs of them: the distinguishing feature of a *yotaka* was a thick layer of white make-up turning the face into a sort of mask. This is probably why in Hiroshige's print the women look like ghosts, something that only intensifies the general gloomy mood of the piece.

The dull, colourless winter landscape accords well with the figures of *yotaka*: in literature and in the fine arts these outcasts were firmly associated with the cold and penetrating damp of winter.

105. The Ommayagashi Embankment

Ommayagashi (12/1857)

The whole of Japan supplied these yards with the timber necessary to build and rebuild after the constant fires to which Edo was prey. The first stores of this kind appeared immediately after it was decided to move the capital to Edo. In the Keicho era (1596-1615) Tokugawa Ieyasu summoned timber merchants, specialists in log-rafting from Suruga and Mikawa provinces. Their yards were constructed in the very centre of the city, on the bank of the Dosanbori canal. The yards were moved several times before, in 1701, it was resolved to shift them to Fukagawa, in the newer part of the city. Two years later the move was complete and Fukagawa kiba ("The Fukagawa Timberyards") appeared on maps of the city. They constantly grew in size, with new plots being bought up and adapted for use by the yard-owners themselves. The logs were mainly stored in man-made ponds connected by canals over an area of a hundred acres.

Timber was transported from the yards to where it was required in rafts, steered by men. Two such rafts are depicted in the print.

Hiroshige presents a specific place here. The composition is based on the sketches he made from life. Yet the view looks like a "winter wonderland". Its "otherworldliness" is enhanced by the emphatic rhythmical composition: the image is enclosed by the logs crossing the picture diagonally and by the lines of the hill descending to the canal. The result is a sort of diamond-shaped frame through which we see the snow-covered banks and trees, the rafts on the water and the dark wintry sky with a sprinkling of falling snow. The "keystone" of this frame takes the form of an open bamboo umbrella bearing the character for "fish" – *uo*, which is the first part of Uoei, the publisher's abbreviated name. His stamp is placed alongside, at the bottom of the left-hand margin.

106. The Fukagawa Timberyards

Fukagawa kiba (8/1856)

Fukagawa Susaki ("the Fukagawa Sandbanks") was the name given to a fairly narrow strip of land along the shore of Edo Bay to the south-east of the timber yards that can be seen on the left-hand edge of the print.

There was a fine view way out to sea from here and the place was regarded as the best for the *hatsuki* ("first sun") ceremony, one of the traditional New Year rituals.

At low-tide edible shellfish could be gathered in the shallows. This shoreline was also a favourite spot for boat-trips in the company of geishas who played musical instruments and sang. In the winter, people came here to watch the sandpipers (*chidori*), small birds indicated here by spots on the surface of the water.

We are looking north-westwards to the area known as Jumantsubo – "One Hundred Thousand Tsubo" (a *tsubo* was roughly four square yards), an area of marshland reclaimed in the 1720s, and Mount Tsukuba on the horizon. In the mid nineteenth century, Jumantsubo contained the suburban residence of one of the *daimyo*. The landscape is deserted and the hand of man only hinted at. The place "belongs" to the gigantic eagle hovering in the winter skies above this vast emptiness.

The bird is symbolic. It is probably an allusion to the deity of the Washi-daimyojin shrine (see No. 101), which by virtue of its location and its main festival, was also linked to the New Year celebrations just like Fukagawa Susaki. On the other hand, it could just be an embodiment of power, decisiveness and might.

107. Susaki and Jumantsubo in Fukagawa

Fukagawa Susaki Jûmantsubo (i5/1857)

Shibaura – "Shiba Coast or Inlet" – is the name of part of the shore of Edo Bay that Hiroshige has already presented in the series (see No. 80).

Here we see the part where the small Shimbashigawa enters the bay. On the southern, man-made sandbar, that covered an area of 60 acres, stood the Hamagoten palace. Its grounds with some buildings are shown on the right, the shoreline reinforced with stone walls.

Originally the palace belonged to a lesser branch of the Tokugawa family, before passing to the ruling line. It remained a residence of the shogun up until the Meiji revolution of 1868.

In 1870 it was converted for the reception of noble foreigners, including guests from Russia.

Beyond the palace grounds, that stick out quite a way into the bay, we see the shoreline of Takanawa and Shinagawa with the new coastal fortifications (*odaiba*) and further towards Haneda.

Freight vessels ply the waters of the bay, keeping to the channel marked by the A-shaped wooden masts. The foreground is occupied by a small flock of *miyakodori*, a variety of sandpiper, found in great numbers around Edo Bay.

108. View of Shibaura Inlet

Shibaura-no fukei (2/1857)

Samezu was the part of the shoreline of Edo Bay, slightly less than a mile long, between the fringes of the Shinagawa district and the mouth of the Tachikawa river. Almost the whole length is shown in the print and, as in many others, the composition is crowned by a majestic mountain, in this case twin-peaked Tsukubayama. Below the mountain, behind the sail of the second ship from us, is the Shinagawa Susaki, a sandbar running out to sea (see No. 83), and beyond it lies Takanawa (see No. 81).

The name Samezu means "Shark Bar" and is associated with an ancient legend. In 1251 a local fisherman caught a shark in his net and in its belly he found a wooden sculpture of Kannon, the bodhisattva of kindness and compassion. The fisherman took the sculpture to Kamakura, then the capital, and presented it to the military government. The head of the government, Hojo Tokiyori (1227-1263), was a pious Buddhist. (He took monastic vows and was known popularly as Saimyoji-dono, "the Lord from Saimyoji", after the Zen Buddhist monastery he founded in Kamakura.) Tokiyori ordered that a Zen monastery be constructed close to the spot where the shark had been caught. It is said that since the monastery appeared on the coast, the sea here has been calm, hence the name Kaianji –

"the Calm Sea Monastery". The chief object of veneration in the monastery was the statue discovered in such a miraculous way and a stone pagoda erected in honour of Tokiyori still stands in the precinct. The monastery became the last resting place of many statesmen, scholars and men of letters of the Edo and early Meiji periods.

As is so often the case in *A Hundred Famous Views of Edo*, the chief feature of the locality is only hinted at: Kaianji lies behind the cluster of trees which form a dark mass at the upper left of the print.

On the west Samezu was bounded by the Tokaido highway, that had already left the city here. Shinagawa was the established "parting place", but sometimes those seeing travellers off went a bit further, to Senzoku. As a result several leisure establishments appeared here, the most famous of which was the Kawasakiya restaurant that still survives today.

The main peculiarity of Samezu was its plantations of *nori*, an edible seaweed. It was grown in a special fashion. In the autumn tree branches were stuck into the shallow bottom in long rows. They became entangled with seaweed as it grew and the harvest could be gathered at low tide in winter and spring. The boats in the foreground are steering between the stands of branches.

109. The Samezu Coast and Minami-Shinagawa

Minami-Shinagawa Samezu kaigan (2/1857)

The pond depicted here was at one time quite extensive, but by the first half of the nineteenth century it had shrunk to three *cho* (about 360 yards) from west to east and 55 yards from north to south. In the depths of a grove on the right bank of the pond we can see the Shinto shrine Senzoku Hachimangu.

This locality is associated with Nichiren (1222-1282), the founder of one of the most popular schools of Buddhism. The pine tree fenced-off on the right bank of the pond is called Kesakakematsu – "the Hanging Robe Pine". Legend has it that Nichiren once stopped to rest beneath this pine and hung his monk's robe (*kesa*) on the tree. A stone memorial plaque was set up by the pine in 1832.

There were several trees with this name in Edo. Two others are well-known: one at Asaji-ga hara in the Asakusa district, the other in the precincts of the Myofukuji monastery in the village of Kamada, the Edogawa district. In all cases the explanation of the name is connected with a prominent Buddhist figure and this probably gave rise to some confusion about the place depicted here. Henry D. Smith II, in particular, identified it with the Myofukuji pine.

110. The "Kesakakematsu Pine" by the Senzoku-no ike Pond

Senzoku-no ike Kesakakematsu (2/1856)

"In olden days there were a great many maples here, and in late autumn when the light of the setting sun fell on their scarlet leaves, it was an exceptionally beautiful sight. Now, however, there are few maples left and only the name remains." That is what *Edo meisho zue* had to say about Yuhinooka, the "Evening Sun Hill", explaining the origin of the name.

The hill (much of which was occupied in the nineteenth century by the suburban residence of the *daimyo* Hosokawa, ruler of Etchu province) was in Meguro, close to the main sight of the district – the Fudo temple, which for reasons that remain unclear Hiroshige did not depict in any of the prints of the series. Behind the hill was a small Buddhist temple called Myooin, approached by the path leading from the bridge on the left. The bridge itself is, however, the semantic and compositional centre of the print.

This is the Taikobashi – "Drum Bridge" – named for its strongly curved shape. There were quite a few bridges of this kind in Edo (see No. 65), but this one was highly unusual because it was built of stone. Despite the fact that stone structures rarely lasted long in Edo with its frequent earthquakes, the bridge in Meguro survived from the 1740s at least into the late 1850s, of which this print is itself proof.

The right-hand approach to the bridge is concealed by the light-grey roof of a lightweight structure on which Hiroshige's signature cartouche is superimposed. This was Shogatsuya noted for its speciality *shiruko-mochi*, a sweet bean-paste soup to which rice cakes were added. This print is very close in mood to Hiroshige's depiction of the Fukagawa timberyards (No. 106). In both instances the calm snow-clad landscape creates an almost symbolic image of nature in its winter lull.

III. The Taikobashi Bridge and Yuhinooka Hill in Meguro

Meguro Taikobashi Yuhinooka (4/1857)

Atagoshita was a place in the Minato district below Mount Atago. The hill is to the right and in the distance we can see the red gate marking the start of the ascent to the Atago-jinja shrine (see No. 21). It was one of the aristocratic areas of the city, containing the mansions of influential *daimyo*. Hiroshige places us here on Yabukoji, but we are looking at another street that runs alongside the Sakuragawa canal near the Zojoji monastery (see No. 79) towards the Toranomon Gate (see No. 113).

The name Yabukoji came from thickets of bamboo and in the right foreground we see the end of a hedge of the great grass.

It marks the boundary of the mansion of the Kato clan, rulers of Minakuchi, a castle town on the Tokaido highway.

A bamboo hedge was considered a magical, as well as practical, protection and was placed on the north-east from which direction demons were supposed to come. The building standing on a platform across the canal is the guardhouse of the mansion.

On the other side of the street we see the mansion of another great feudal lord – Hijikata, the *daimyo* of Komono.

This print is among the most celebrated winter snow scenes in *A Hundred Famous Views of Edo*.

112. Yabukoji Lane at Atagoshita

Atagoshita Yabukoji (12/1857)

The Toranomon Gate stood in the very centre of Edo, close to Kasumigaseki (see No. 3) and the Outer Moat of the castle. The name means "Tiger Gate" and, as is often the case, there are various explanations for it. It may be connected with a sweet-smelling cherry tree called Toranoo ("Tiger's Tail") that grew alongside the Naito clan mansion inside the shogun's castle, of which the Toranomon was the outer gate. According to a different version, the gate was once used by a Korean embassy that brought a caged tiger as a diplomatic gift. The cage was so large that the gate had to be dismantled to let it pass and when the gate was rebuilt it was named in commemoration of this event.

Whatever the case, Toranomon was built in 1614 and stood until 1873. The print, as its title suggests, shows not the gate itself, but the adjoining locality, primarily the Aoizaka or "Mallow Slope". The tree at the top is one of the *enoki*, iron-trees, that grew in large numbers here and gave their name to another slope that runs leftwards from this tree.

The slope runs alongside the spillway of the Tameike pond (see No. 52) which links it with the Sotobori (Outer Moat). On the right side of the spillway we see the buildings of Sanno-jinja - one of the oldest and most popular Shinto shrines in the Eastern Capital. It was founded by Ota Dokan (1432-1486), the first builder of Edo and from the start was intended to protect the city from demons. The shrine retained its supposed function during the Keicho era (1596-1615). Tokugawa Ieyasu, the new master of Edo, transferred it to another site in the Kojimachi quarter. It was moved to its present site in 1659. The shrine was dear to the hearts of the ordinary people on account of Sanno-matsuri, Edo's most beloved temple festival. The shrine itself is an indisputable landmark of the locality and its detailed representation might well have been provided as the subject of this print. In this print, however, it is another shrine - Konpira - which "provides the plot".

The two young men in the foreground are dressed rather unsuitably for the winter, wearing nothing but loincloths and headscarfs. They are performing a seasonal ritual known as *kan-mairi* - "pilgrimage in the bitter cold". This was originally an ascetic practice among monks: in the winter months, particularly at the time of *daikan*, the "Great Cold" that came in the middle of the Second Month, the monks poured cold water over themselves and went about the streets dressed in light linen clothing, chanting prayers to the accompaniment of a gong. This custom appeared in the early eighteenth century. By the start of the following century, it was rarely performed by monks, but increasingly popular with the laity, especially craftsmen. Eventually it became a compulsory element of the ten-year apprenticeship.

For thirty days on end, in the depths of winter, the apprentices were expected to go out at dusk dressed as we see them here. They went to a shrine or monastery where they performed a ritual of purification, dousing themselves with icy water, and offered up prayers for achieving perfection in their chosen trade. Then they paraded through the dark streets, lighting their way with lanterns as they recited prayers and rang a bell.

The apprentices here are of different ages. The one in front is twelve or thirteen and has just entered the workshop; the other is about ten years older and approaching the end of his learning years. They are returning from the Konpira shrine, as can be seen from the inscription on the younger one's lantern: *Konpira Daigongen*.

Despite the cold and the dark of evening, the slope is fairly busy with people going up and down by lantern-light. Two "mobile snack-bars" are plying for trade. Each has its speciality written on a lantern covered with red paper. The far one is selling noodles made from buck-wheat flour; the other offers more elaborate fare - *ohira-shippoku* - noodles garnished with finely chopped fried egg, mushrooms, fish and so on.

This is one of the most attractive winter scenes in Hiroshige's series. It combines all possible means of characterizing a given locality: topographic, seasonal, emotional and - something often missing in the winter views - ethnographic.

113. The Aoizaka Slope beyond the Toranomon Gate

Toranomon-soto Aoizaka (11/1857)

This bridge stood in the very centre of Edo, spanning the Kyobashi river at the point where it flowed into the Sotobori, the Outer Moat of the castle. The bridge was in the very heart of Edo's commercial and manufacturing life, yet the immediate area had a rather dubious reputation reflected in the name of the bridge.

Literally it means "Nuns' Bridge", but the *bikuni* referred to were low-class prostitutes, one small step up from the *yotaka* (see No. 105). They got this colloquial name because they dressed like Buddhist nuns. They plied their trade in mean houses of assignation, of which there were a particularly large number in the vicinity of this bridge.

Hiroshige depicts an ordinary, everyday scene of city life here. In the distance we see a fire-watchtower, an invariable feature of the Eastern Capital, particularly near the centre.

The foreground is occupied by two eating-houses. On the right is a stall with an inscribed lantern announcing that it sells sweet potato rissoles (*imo*). Hot sweet potatoes was the simplest kind of fare, but everyone enjoyed it, especially in wintertime. Alongside we can see the wheel of the cart on which the stall will be loaded and taken away at the end of the working day. Opposite is a more permanent establishment whose sign promises *yamakujira* – "mountain whale", a euphemism for the meat of various wild animals.

In the first half of the Edo period the Buddhist prohibition on eating meat was strictly enforced, but later things gradually became laxer. Places like this one offered dishes made from wild boar and venison, as well as more unusual animals: bear, monkey, raccoon-dog (*tanuki*), otter, wolf, fox and weasel.

114. The Bikunibashi Bridge in a Snow Shower

Bikunibashi seishû (10/1858)

Edo appeared as a military city and samurai made up at least half of its population. Times changed. Under the Tokugawa dynasty Japan entered a prolonged period of peace. The moral and professional degeneration of the martial class became a danger and the government devoted much attention to instilling in the samurai the ethical standards of the *bushido*, the "way of the warrior" and maintaining their military preparedness. With this aim several riding grounds were created in Edo. The first was Takata-no baba constructed in 1636 in a north-western suburb of the Eastern Capital. Throughout the Edo period it was used not only for ordinary training, but also for displays of archery on horseback, shooting at a fixed target (*yabusame*).

This custom, which appeared in Japan back in the Heian period (794-1125), was always accompanied by a solemn religious service for peace in the country.

Hiroshige's print depicts samurai training at Takata-no baba. In the center two horsemen gallop towards each other. To the right of them, three archers stripped to the waist, practice shooting at a round target which is depicted right in the foreground. The tips of the arrows were wrapped in cloth, so that they bounced off the leather-covered target. Takata-no baba was also connected with the story of the forty-seven *ronin*. One of these loyal vassals, Horibe Yasubei (1670-1703), took part in a battle here that became the subject of tales and *Kabuki* plays.

115. The Takata Riding Ground

Takata-no baba (2/1857)

This low-lying area, made up mostly of rice paddies, adjoined the Kanda-josui aqueduct seen in the foreground. The aqueduct is crossed by the Omokagehashi – the "Bridge of Reflections". The name is connected with a legend that in the fifteenth century Otohime, the wife of Kokawa Yoshiharu, grieving for her murdered husband, drowned herself when she saw his image undulating on the surface of the water. The name "Sugataminohashi" (which can also be translated as "Bridge of Reflections") included in the title of the print might apply to the small plank bridge visible on the centre right, or it may be simply an alternative name for the larger bridge.

The plank bridge led to the Shinto shrine of Hikawa-myojinsha, the entrance to which is marked by a *torii* gate.

The shrine was built in 1730 on the orders of Shogun Tokugawa Yoshimune. It was held to protect the surrounding locality, but its popularity was as much due to the fact that in front of it was a semi-legal "green quarter" served by courtesans of an inferior kind. By Hiroshige's time, this was in the past and the area was occupied by restaurants, teahouses and an archery-stand.

Opposite stands the Shingon Buddhist monastery Nanzenji, founded at the start of the sixteenth century and around it the houses of the village of Jariba ("Gravel Quarry"), whose name suggests that it was constructed on a bar of shingles. This print is among the "topographic" views in the series where the details of the locality are presented with particular precision and are easily recognizable.

116. The Sugataminohashi Bridge, Omokagenohasohi Bridge and the Jariba Quarter

Omokagenohashi Jâriba (1/1857)

Here we are back in the very centre of old Edo, looking at the Shinobazu-no ike Pond (see No. 11) in the middle of which was the famous shrine of Benzaiten, the water deity and goddess of happiness. On the opposite bank we can see the red buildings of Kanyeiji.

Hiroshige places us alongside the red torii gate marking the entrance to a shrine dedicated to the deified scholar and minister of the Heian period Sugawara Michizane (845-903). The shrine was called Yushima Tenjin or Yushima Temmangu.

Michizane was venerated as a god of thunder, but more importantly as the patron deity of scholars, writers, poets and students. Temmangu at Yushima was among the oldest shrines in Edo. It was founded back in 1355, although originally dedicated to a different deity. It became linked with Michizane the following century, in 1478, by Ota Dokan (1432-1486) after he appeared to him in a dream. It was Dokan too who planted hundreds of cherry trees in the area for which the shrine is still famous today.

Yushima Tenjin was surrounded by teahouses (the red lanterns of one of them can be seen to the right of the *torii*), restaurants, houses of assignation, and the like. But the citizens of Edo were drawn most of all by the *tomikuji* (lottery) - a game of chance in a country where they were only permitted on exceptional occasions. Among those occasions was the fair in the precincts of the shrine which was held twice a month. It attracted so many visitors that children were repeatedly getting lost in the crowd. This became such a regular occurrence that in 1850 a special rectangular pillar was set up for announcements. Notices describing lost children were stuck on one side, those describing children that had been found on the other. The pillar still exists.

Two flights of steps led to the top of the hill on which the shrine stood. The gentler climb was known as the "female slope", the other as the "male slope". In Hiroshige's print the former comes up from the pond, the latter from the right. A stone at the top of the "male slope" gives its name - Otokozaka.

117. View from the Tenjin Shrine Hill at Yushima

Yushima Tenjin sakaue tenbo (4/1856)

This print stands apart from the rest of the series. It depicts neither a monastery, nor a shrine or a hill, waterfall or bridge. It does not depict any festival, although the subject is related to the chief festival of all four seasons – the New Year, more precisely its approach. This print draws the balance of the series but at the same time, Edo is presented in a "strange" aspect: the artist plunges into the world of ghosts and transformed creatures, the realm beyond.

The locality depicted is admittedly, quite real. It is an area adjoining the quarter (or village) called Shozokumachi (whose buildings can be seen at the edge of the field) some 400 yards east of the Oji Inari-gongen shrine (see No. 18). The spot was called Shozoku-bata (Shozoku Fields). Both the settlement and the field are quite recognizable, but the subject of the print is not them, but the belief that gave them their name. It is the *enoki*, iron-tree, standing in the centre and the host of vixens accompanied by mysterious tongues of flame (*kitsunebi*).

In Japan, the vixen was considered a malevolent creature, fond of causing people trouble. They were depicted in this light, particularly at the moment of transformation and most often, made to appear sinister and somewhat caricature-like. Here, however, they have a different appearance. Their poses are solemn, their movements gracious and restrained. They are carrying out their main ritual of the year and preparing to assume the guise of noble ladies.

The original gathering point was not the iron-tree but the adjacent pine, which Hiroshige also depicted. However, in all likelihood at the start of the nineteenth century, the function was attributed to its more unusually shaped neighbour. The belief still lives on today, but now, of course, it is attached to yet another, relatively young tree. It was planted about 1830 and survived the bombing of April 1945 that devastated the whole area, but miraculously left this tree untouched.

118. "Fox Fires" by the Iron-Tree at Oji

Oji Shôzoku enoki omisoka no kitsunebi (9/1857)

Aizome – a dark blue dye used in the 18th and 19th centuries to apply designs to light summer kimonos, towels, etc.

Akane – madder, a perennial plant the root of which was used to produce a red-dye stuff.

Amigasa – a wide-brimmed conical hat woven from straw and sedge and worn as a protection from the sun.

Atake-bune – literally, "brave ship". A large battle ship used in the second half of the 16th century and the first half of the 17th. It was propelled by 50 to 80 oarsmen.

Bakufu – the military government of Japan between the late 12th century and 1868.

Bijin-ga – literally, "a depiction of beauties". One of principal genres in the Japanese woodblock print. The models were mainly beautiful women, residents of the "pleasure quarters" in Edo.

Bikuni – a Buddhist nun.

Bodaiji – a monastery incorporating a necropolis of several generations of one family or clan.

Bonten – a festive pole decorated with fabric, paper and cords.

Bushido – literally, "the way of the warrior". The moral codex of the samurai. The *bushido* doctrine began to take shape in the Kamakura period (1185-1333) and took its final form based on the neo-Confucian teaching, during the Edo period (1613-1868).

Chidori – sandpiper.

Chokibune – small narrow boats with upturned prows reminiscent of a wild boar's tusk (*choki*), hence the name. They served as fishing, transport and pleasure boats.

Chonin – city dwellers. The society of the Edo period was divided into the four estates: the samurai, peasants, craftsmen and merchants. The latter two were united in the *chonin* category. The culture of the third and fourth estates, *chonin-no bunka*, became the most remarkable phenomenon in the culture of the Edo period (1613-1868).

Daikan – literally, "great cold". The coldest season in Japan which comes about the end of January.

Daikon – large radish used as a piquant sauce.

Daimyo – literally, "great name". During the Edo period, senoir figures in the feudal hierarchy governing large territories and subordinate directly to the *shogun* (qv.), the military ruler of Japan.

Dango – a dumpling made with rice flour.

Danjiri – decoratively designed four-wheel cart used in festive processions; the same as *sansha*.

Dengaku – *tofu* (qv.) boiled with *miso* (qv.).

Edokko – native-born residents of Edo.

Egoyomi – an illustrated calendar in which long and short months according to the Far Eastern calendar are indicated. When such a calendar was produced directly by a publishing-house, the publisher carefully concealed the fact because the private publication of calendars was prohibited.

Ema – a representation of a horse. A votive offering to a temple. It is believed that such depictions of horses took the place of real horses originally used. Though, during the Edo period the subject matter of ema was not limited to horses. They could feature famous warriors, actors, beauties and even notorious villains. The name, however, remained unchanged.

Enoki – iron-tree.

Ezo – an ancient name of the island of Hokkaido, as well as of its inhabitants, the Ainu.

Fujidana – a pergola entwined with climbing fuji, wistaria, which looks particularly beautiful during the flowering period (May and June) when the blooms hang down from the wooden trellising.

Fuji-zuka – a man-made hill in imitation of Fujiyama. Such places were used by associations of pilgrims (*fujiko*) for ritual ascensions instead of a pilgrimage to a real Fuji.

Fukei-ga – a landscape genre in the Japanese woodblock print.

Fukura-suzume – literally, "sparrow of happiness". The representation had a benevolent character. The symbolism of the representation is based on the play on words: the word *fukura* can be understood literally as "fat", "swollen" or as *fuku*, "happiness", and *ra* – a pluralizing suffix. Thus the representation of a sparrow with fluffed up feathers turned into a propitiatory symbol.

Funeasobi – an entertainment on water; boating, often in the company of geishas who sang and performed for passengers.

Furoshiki – a coloured kerchief used to wrap various objects for carrying them.

Geta – high wooden sandals on a thick sole with two or three supports.

Giboshi – literally, "false pearl". An onion-shaped decorative finial of bridge rails. The name derives from a sacred attribute in Buddhist painting, the *chintamani* pearl, which had a similar shape.

Gidayu-bushi – a kind of theatricalized story-telling which evolved in Kyoto during the Genroku era (1688-1704). It was introduced by Takemoto Gidayu (1691-1744), hence the name.

Gogatsu-nobori – literally, "May banner". A banner of any form, usually in the shape of carp, which was hoisted on a tall pole on the 5th day of the Fifth Month, the Day of Boys.

Gohei – ornamental arrangements of paper strips of cut paper used in Shinto rituals.

Gosekku – the five traditional Japanese holidays: *jinjitsu* (literally, "man's day") on the 7th day of the First Month; *joshi* – the Festival of Girls on the 3rd day of the Third Month; *tango* – the Festival of Boys on the 5th day of the Fifth Month; *tanabatamatsuri* – the Festival of the Ox-herd and the Weaver-Girl on the 7th day of the Seventh Month; and *tee* – the Festival of Chrysanthemums on the 9th day of the Ninth Month.

Gumbai – literally, "military fan". A non-folding fan made of iron and leather in the shape of a gourd. It was used as a military leader's staff.

Hachimaki – a headband tied on the forehead with a knot similar in shape to the character for "eight" (*hachi*), hence its name.

Hagoita – a kind of racket used in the game of battle-dore and shuttlecock. It was one of traditional New-Year presents. One side of a presentation piece used to be decorated with painting or appliqué work on a variety of subjects, mostly depictions of famous beauties or actors.

Hanabi – fireworks. Fireworks were very popular with Edoans. Especially popular were *hanabi* on the Sumidagawa, near the Ryogokubashi bridge during the Opening of the River festival.

Hanagasa – literally, "flower hat". A hat decorated with real or artificial flowers, an indispenable attribute of many festivities.

Hanami – contemplation of flowers. The ceremony of admiring cherry blossom in spring, a traditional seasonal pastime.

Hanashobu – a flower related to the iris, scientific name, *iris kaempferi*.

Hannoki – a Japanese variety of alder.

Haori – a cloak, part of a costume used for ceremonial occasions.

Hatamoto – literally, "standard-bearer". A samurai of a high rank, a direct vassal of the *shogun* (qv.).

Hatsugatsuo – the first catch of mackerel. The catching of mackerel began in spring, during the Fourth Month. The first mackerel, regarded as a delicacy, was very expensive.

Hibachi – a brazier with coals installed in a room so that people, sitting around it, could warm themselves.

Hibutsu – literally, "secret Buddha". The most revered deity in a Buddhist monastery, its protector. It is called "secret" because the image is usually on display, but kept in a *zushi* (qv.) opened on special festive days.

Hirokoji – the widening out of a street intended to form a firebreak hindering the rapid spread of a conflagration. This was very important in Edo, a megapolis of wooden structures.

Hishaku – a ladle for water made of bamboo, wood or metal. It was used both in everyday life and during the tea ceremony.

Hojoe – the festival of releasing birds, fish and turtles on the 15th day of the Eighth Month. The ceremony is of Buddhist origin.

Honden – the principal building of a Shinto shrine.

Hondo – the main temple of a Buddhist monastery.

Honsha – the main shrine of the Shinto cult.

Honzon – a depiction of the main deity in a Buddhist monastery.

Hotokedana – literally, "a strip for buddhas". A home altar where images of buddhas and boddhisattvas were placed.

Hozuki – Chinese lantern plant.

Hyotan – a bottle gourd. A vegetable with a narrow neck in the middle used as a bottle for water, wine or medicine. The gourd was an attribute of sennins, Taoist immortals. It was believed that they used gourds to store an elixir of immortality.

Junishi – literally, "twelve branches". The twelve year names of the 60-year cycle according to the Oriental calendar. In combination with the "ten stems" reflecting the connection of a year with one of the five elements (wood, fire, earth, metal and water), they make up a complete designation of the year in this cycle. However, a year is usually indicated in abbreviated form, using the names of the "stems" – the Year of the Tiger, the Year of the Snake, etc.

Kadomatsu – literally, "a pine by the gate". Traditional New Year decoration consisting of pine-tree branches, pieces of bamboo stem and various objects having a propitiatory message.

Kago – a variety of palanquin carried by two men on their shoulders with the help of a squared beam passed through the cover.

Kagura – ritual music and dances performed in Shinto shrines.

Kaicho – literally, "the opening of a reliquary". The display in Buddhist shrines of the statues of particularly revered deities, ordinarily in *zushi* (qv.)

Kannushi – a Shinto priest.

Kariginu – literally, "hunter's clothes". Originally this garment was indeed used for hunting, but in the Heian period (794-1185) such loose clothing which did not constrain movements became the everyday costume of aristocrats.

Kawabiraki – literally, "the opening of the river". The festival on the River

Sumidagawa near the Ryogokubashi bridge in Edo celebrated on the 28th day of the Fifth Month and accompanied with fireworks.

Kesa – a Buddhist's monk's robe worn over one shoulder so that the other remains bare.

Kodan – a popular tale, a variety of public speech. Story-tellers, *kodanshi*, performed in streets and attracted large audiences. The subjects were commonly historical events interpreted in a dramatic manner. The historical knowledge of the inhabitants of Edo in the 18th and 19th centuries was largely derived from *kodan* tales.

Kosatsuba – site with stands for the display of decrees and public announcements.

Kumade – literally, "bear's claw". A special rake, made in a variety of sizes, with all sorts of amulets attached to it, in particular the mask of Ame-no Uzume, the goddess of happiness. The *kumade* was an indispensable attribute and souvenir of a general Edo festival, Tori-no ichi, the "Hen's Market" which was held on the first day of the Hen of the Eleventh Month near the Washi-jinja shrine in the Shitaya district of Edo.

Machibugyo – a government position during the Edo period, the mayor of a town. There were two machibugyo in Edo governing different parts of the city.

Megane-e – literally, "spectacles pictures". Engravings and pictorial representations intended for viewing with a special device – *nozoki-karakuri* (peep show), which made the representation more life-like through a system of mirrors and special light effects.

Meisho – literally, "landmark". A landscape genre in the Japanese woodblock print.

Miko – priests of a Shinto shrine who performed ritual dances and made prophecies.

Mikoshi – a sacred palanquin, a reliquary containing the holy objects of a Shinto shrine. An indispensable attribute of a shrine's festive procession.

Minogame – a mythological turtle living for a long time. After 10,000 years, it was believed to grow a long tail by which the *minogame* could be identified. In the fine arts the turtle was a firmly established symbol – a wish for longevity.

Miso – a dense mass of fermented beans used as a sauce and for making soups.

Mochi – rice cakes.

Mombi – a festive, specific day. In "pleasure quarters", such a holiday was quite the opposite for its female residents. Unlike ordinary days, during a *mombi* courtesans had no right to refuse their favours to anybody.

Momen – cotton fabric.

Momiji – scarlet maple leaves. The process of admiring them (*momijigiri*) was one of seasonal entertainments.

Nagaya – literally, "long house". Large apartment houses in major Japanese cities during the Edo period. A *nagaya* consisted of small separate apartments each having its own entrance. Usually they were rented out. The majority of the inhabitants of Edo lived in *nagaya*.

Noren – an awning hung at the entrance to a shop, usually carrying its owner's trademark.

Nori – edible seaweeds.

Nozoki-karakuri – see *megane-e*.

Ogi – folding fan. Unlike the *uchiwa*, the rigid fan of Chinese origin, the ogi was a Japanese invention. It is believed that such fans came into common use during the Heian period (794-1185).

Okabasho – those "pleasure quarters" in Edo which, unlike the "licensed" Yoshiwara quarters, had no official sanction from the government. Okabasho quarters were situated mainly in the Fukagawa, Tsukiji, Shinagawa and Shinjuku districts of Edo.

Ramma – a board between the ceiling and the lintel (*kamoi*) decorated with an openwork design and wooden reliefs. It was one of the principal decorative elements used both in religious edifices and dwelling houses during the Tokugawa period.

Rangaku – "Dutch scholarship". A trend in Japanese culture of the Edo period. It took shape in the Kyoho era (1716-1736) after the government revoked the law prohibiting the import and study of European (Dutch) scholarly works. The *rangakusha* scholars studied Dutch and translated works devoted to botany, anatomy, geography, etc. The artists of the Dutch trend copied European etchings, especially book illustrations, and, mastering in this way the light-and-shade modelling of form and the linear perspective, created their own works with the use of these devices. A distinctive Dutch-oriented movement known as *rangaku-e* evolved in Japanese painting. Its major representative was Shiba Kokan (1747-1818).

Ronin – a masterless samurai.

Sashimi – a dish prepared of raw fish cut in slices, with a piquant sauce.

Sennin (Chinese Hsien) – a Taoist immortal.

Senryu – a seventeen-syllable humorous poem. Unlike other poetic forms, the *senryu* used everyday vocabulary and vernacular idiom. As a rule, *senryu* poems had a complex, many-layered message which made them similar to a rebus. The process of deciphering was an important moment in the appreciation of a *senryu*.

Shamisen – a three-string musical instrument with a long finger-board and a resonator covered with cat's skin. It was brought to Japan from China or possibly from the Ryukyu Islands during the Eiroku era (1558-1570).

Shichifukujin – the Seven Gods of Happiness. A group of gods which was most

revered in Japanese popular beliefs and included Buddhist, Shinto and Taoist personages.

Shimenawa – a sacred cord used in Shinto rituals to drive away evil spirits. It was woven of straw and decorated with bunches of grass and *kamishide*, decorative paper figures.

Shinden – a Shinto temple, one of the three buildings making up a Shinto shrine.

Shishi – a mythological animal, usually translated as "lion". Their representations are often placed in front of Buddhist temples and Shinto shrines.

Shishimai – a dance which came from China and was performed by an actor wearing a *shishi* (qv.) mask.

Shita-e – a sketch in ink often not worked out in detail, which was produced by the painter as a sketch for a woodblock print. As a rule, later the *shita-e* was given to the master who created the *han-shitae*, "painting for a woodblock" from which the image, already in finished form, was transferred to the woodblock and printed.

Shobu – a variety of iris.

Shogun – the military ruler of Japan. Between 1185 and 1868 shoguns from three successive dynasties (Minamoto, Ashikaga and Tokugawa) ruled the country.

Shoji – movable partitions dividing rooms in a Japanese house, especially those separating the inner rooms from the engawa, the gallery overlooking the garden. They were made of wood and lined with an opaque matt paper.

Soba – soup containing noodles made with buck-wheat flour.

Soroban – a Japanese abacus.

Sumo – a variety of Japanese wrestling. Originally competition between of *sumo* wrestlers had a ritual character and for a long time they were held in Shinto shrines.

Sushi – boiled rice cakes plastered over with raw fish and flavoured with a specially prepared soya bean sauce.

Takarabune – literally, "a treasure ship". A symbolic painted, printed or sculpted representation of a ship with its prow in the shape of a dragon's head. Its crew consisted of *shichifu-kujin* (qv.) and its load included various propitiatory objects – symbols of wealth, longevity, high rank, etc. Takarabune representations were usually put at the head of the bed during the first night of the New Year. It was believed that this would make the first dream, thought to be decisive for the whole year, a happy one.

Tanzaku – a strip of paper with poems written on it. Sometimes the paper itself was decorated with various patterns.

Tengu – a mountain spirit. A mythological creature of Chinese origin, which was substantially transformed in Japan. During the Edo period tengu were depicted as long-nosed men or bird-like creatures. They occur in many legends and works of fiction.

Tenka-matsuri – (also *Sanno-matsuri*), the festival of the Hieshi-jinja shrine. One of the few urban festivities during which a procession was admitted to the *shogun*'s castle area and viewed by him, or those close to him.

Tofu – bean curds.

Tomikuji – a lottery, a kind of the game of chance. It was forbidden more than once during the Edo period.

Tori-eboshi – a variety of hat worn on ceremonial occasions.

Torii – a distinctively shaped gateway of wood or stone placed at the entrance to the Shinto shrine.

Tozama-daimyo – known as "outer *daimyo*"; the feudal landlords of the Edo period who were not the *shogun*'s kin or his immediate vassals.

Ukiyo-e – literally, "pictures of the floating world". Paintings and coloured woodblock prints of everyday life particularly popular in the Edo period (1615-1867).

Umeboshi – pickled plums.

Waraji – straw shoes.

Yaezakura – a cherry tree of the double-blossomed variety. It blossoms somewhat later than other varieties.

Yakatabune – a large covered pleasure boat intended for entertainments on a river.

Yakusha-e – a depiction of actors; a print of the theatrical genre.

Yamabiraki – literally, "the opening of a mountain". The season of pilgrimages to sacred mountains, e.g. Mount Fuji.

Yamabushi – wandering Buddhist monks of the Shugendo school.

Yamakago – literally, "mountain palanquin". A special light palanquin intended for travel along mountain roads and other difficult routes.

Yanebune – a covered pleasure boat.

Yujo – a general name for various kinds of courtesans.

Yukata – a light summer cotton kimono.

Zashiki – the main reception room in a traditional Japanese home or a general room in a pleasure house.

Zushi – a reliquary; an upright lacquered wooden box, in which the image of a Buddhist deity is kept. *Zushi* vary in shape – small ones were intended for domestic worship, while in monasteries they could reach a height of seven feet to accommodate large statues.